INVESTIGATING STAGE HYPNOSIS

The Author

Tracie O'Keefe, BA, N-SHAP Adv Dip Thp MCRAH is a Clinical hypnotherapist, Psychotherapist and Counsellor at the London Medical Centre in Harley Street. After being issued with a writ for libel by one of England's most famous stage hypnotists in 1996, for commenting on his stage show, she decided it was time to warn members of the public of the dangers of stage hypnosis.

Katrina Fox (Editor) is a freelance journalist and editor, and the co-author of *Trans-X-U-All: The Naked Difference*.

I DEDICATE THIS BOOK TO

ALL THE PEOPLE DAMAGED BY
THE STAGE HYPNOSIS PROCESS

TRUST AGAIN, FOR HELP IS AT
HAND

INVESTIGATING STAGE HYPNOSIS

Tracie O'Keefe

Edited by Katrina Fox

Published by:
Extraordinary People Press
Suite 412 Triumph House
185-191 Regent Street
London W1R 7WB
Tel. 0171 734 3749
Fax. 0171 439 3536
E-mail katfox@easynet.co.uk
Web site http://easyweb.easynet.co.uk/~katfox/

First published 1998

British Library Cataloguing-in-Publication Data
A catalogue record for this book is available from the
British Library

ISBN 0 9529482 1 4

Printed by the Ipswich Book Company, Ipswich, Great
Britain

Distributed in the UK by Turnaround

**"No matter where you go
You go in your own mind"**

Katrina Fox 1997

By the same author:

**Trans-X-U-All: The Naked Difference
(with Katrina Fox 1997)**

Published by Extraordinary People Press
ISBN 0 9529482 0 6

CONTENTS

Acknowledgements

Thanks to:

The staff at the:
London University for their careful and devoted care of the Harry Price collection of historical references to hypnotism.
Theatre Museum, Covent Garden for their useful cuttings on stage hypnosis.
British Broadcasting Corporation, whose television archives were invaluable.

Alan Gauld, whose seminal work *The History of Hypnotism* was a great source of information.

My tutors and supervisors over the years, for all their knowledge and help.

Special thanks to:

Derek Crussell, the south London hypnotherapist, who has helped the victims of stage hypnosis for years and who provided me with information, always with a kind word and for whom nothing was ever too much to ask.

Margaret Harper and her family and friends, who run the Campaign Against Stage Hypnosis and who diligently supplied me with many of the newspaper cuttings and documents I needed for this book.

Michael Joseph and the staff at the *European Journal of Clinical Hypnosis* for their integrity, help and advice

Katrina Fox, my untiring partner and editor, for her infinitesimal patience and without whom this project would remain a pile of notes and scribblings.

Foreword

My introduction to the world of stage hypnosis was a particularly tragic one when my daughter Sharron died only hours after taking part as a volunteer in a show. My family have always felt that she would not have been dead the next morning had she not been involved in this practice that passes for entertainment. At the time we did not understand what was happening at the inquest and ever since we have had to fight for the recognition that she did not die of natural causes.

During the past four years, since her death, hundreds of letters have landed on my doormat from many people, who have also been hurt and abused by stage hypnotists. These people have all said that they were not warned of the dangers before they took part in the show, but even sadder is the fact that their complaints were rarely taken seriously. The sheer mystery and elusiveness of stage hypnosis made it impossible for other people to understand the pain they suffered and had to deal with, often years after the show.

We need a better understanding of stage hypnosis and how dangerous it is for people to be involved in what seems to be nothing more than a bit of fun. This excellent and illuminating book I hope will help both the public and professionals in hypnosis to be more informed. We have been fed on a diet of lies and half-truths about stage hypnosis, which has created confusion. In the meantime even more volunteers are still suffering damage to their health and minds.

Tracie O'Keefe has written a powerful and revealing exposé that I am confident will go a long way to promoting a greater understanding of the issues surrounding stage hypnosis, even though there are some who would rather she had stayed silent.

Margaret Harper, Founder of the Campaign Against Stage Hypnosis (CASH), November 1997

Preface

As I sit down to write this book I am aware that is not me writing it at all, but a representation of events unfolding that need to be recorded. I find myself a knight in the battle against the dangerous practice of stage hypnosis, having been issued with a writ for libel by someone whose show I commented on. As the battle heats up I want to say it is not the people that practise stage hypnosis that I have anything against, but the practice itself.

When you first look at the antics going on in a stage hypnosis show they seem to be harmless and everyone appears to be having fun. Looking closer it becomes evident that stage hypnotists are often either not sure about what they are doing or carelessly damaging people as they play for belly laughs to the stalls, sometimes for enormous fees.

The stage hypnotists' subjects do things like starting to take their clothes off, pretending to be washing machines, kissing members of the audience, or forgetting their own names and perhaps even believing they are Napoleon. The illusion is created that the stage hypnotist has power over people's minds and bodies and this causes them to humiliate themselves in front of their friends, sometimes against their will.

In the worst cases people have died after the event or been committed to a mental institution to receive long-term psychiatric care. Others have reported disturbances of sleep or behaviour patterns that can last for years. Included in this book are reports from the victims themselves, in their own words, telling us of the traumas they have suffered after being volunteers in stage hypnosis shows.

I promise to open my mouth wide, exposing hypocrisy, and validating the caring use of hypnosis as being separate. The investigations and information within these pages aim to clarify the issues surrounding the practice of stage hypnosis, leaving the reader with no doubt about the realities, truths and dangers.

Tracie O'Keefe, December 1997

1

Defining Stage Hypnosis for Entertainment Purposes

All over the world many theatres, clubs, pubs, bars and television stations present stage hypnosis shows, where the hypnotist, who appears to be of magician-like status, puts the volunteers into a trance and induces them to act out an endless, obedient charade.

In recent years stage hypnosis has got a great deal of bad press, which may be justified but is certainly not new. Since the beginning of stage hypnosis shows in our modern Western culture the healing professions have been opposed to the use of hypnosis for entertainment. They believe that it demeans and misuses this powerful tool, presenting it in a light of trivia and folly. Furthermore the healing professions also believe that many stage hypnotists are badly trained, if trained at all, and that they not only create health problems in their subjects, but could even cause death.

Over the past decade the press has carried many stories of people who claim to have had their lives disturbed after having been the victims of stage hypnotists' incompetence. These complaints can vary from a few days of dizziness, through to change of sexual motivation, psychosis and in some cases Sudden Death Syndrome. When the new wave of stage hypnosis came to the public's attention, from the early 1980s onwards, the sensationalist headlines describing the damage to some of the subjects followed closely behind.

It is not without due cause that the public, who have become more comfortable with hypnosis in recent years, are now beginning to view it again with suspicion. As hypnosis is being recognised all over the world as a useful tool for the professional healthcare worker, social worker and teacher, there is a need for those professions to clearly define the line of separation between themselves and stage hypnotists.

The stage hypnotist is a showperson; their job is to entertain, and the long-term mental welfare of the subjects is not of the highest priority. The added danger is that the stage hypnotist may have no training in mental health and may not truly be aware of or understand the possible consequences of their actions. They work as a theatrical entertainer and not a mental health professional. Some of them have not even had any training and have learnt hypnosis from a book.

A stage hypnotist requires no qualifications, has to pass no test or examination and requires no licence to perform. In certain places they may need to inform the local authority and attain a permit, but this is easily done and very few questions are asked. The permit involved is actually for public entertainment and anyone calling themselves a stage hypnotist may apply for it.

At the beginning of the show the stage hypnotist knows how to build their act and induce trust in the majority of the audience. Although they have no qualifications they will often make references to "My close friend Dr X". Another trick is to tell the audience about their many professional appearances and how many people they have hypnotised over the years. This is what is called validation by association and although an individual may have no qualifications themselves, they associate themselves with qualified and trustworthy archetypes.

The audience, however, knows nothing of hypnosis and trusts the hypnotist, who has billed themselves along the lines of "Merlin The Great", to have a reasonable idea about what they are doing. The vast majority of the audiences who attend hypnosis shows have no idea that the hypnotist may have only learnt their craft from a book; they are the unsuspecting public who are already relying on the hypnotist's illusion of his or her own importance and abilities being true.

The principle of Caveat Emptor (buyer beware) applies

So who monitors stage hypnotists? The truth is, no one. Local authorities who issue entertainment licences to permit them to perform, have no knowledge of hypnosis. If there are statutory restrictions they often prove impossible to enforce, since they are either too loosely framed to have any effect or no one in that local authority understands their meaning. Few politicians want to be seen as killjoys, prohibiting their constituents from having a good time being entertained by stage hypnosis; their priority, after all, is getting re-elected through being as popular as possible.

No one likes a killjoy.

The average person, who knows nothing of hypnosis, often sees no difference between stage hypnotists and clinical hypnotists. The art of clinical hypnosis, used by many hypnotherapists, psychotherapists, doctors, psychologists, psychiatrists and accelerated learning teachers becomes tarnished simply by association when stage hypnotists cause damage to their subjects.

I cannot tell you that I wrote this book to define the line which clearly separates those professionals from the stage hypnotists. Nor can I just show you that stage hypnosis needs to be scrutinised by governments, cultures and professional clinicians. All I have done in this book is to give a voice to the opinions, information, and evidence, which were just waiting to be co-ordinated.

In 1996 *The New Encyclopedia of Stage Hypnotism* by Ormond McGill was published by The Anglo American Book Company. It is the culmination of a lifetime's knowledge of stage hypnosis recorded by the author. A man into his 80s, McGill has spent many years practising stage hypnosis in various forms, entertaining the American public through stage and television. His book seemed to be an update of an earlier work, *The Encyclopedia of Genuine Stage Hypnotism*, published by Abbott's Magic Company of Colon, Michigan, USA, in 1947.

As far as stage hypnosis goes the book is a compendium for instructing the would-be performer. It does, however, give a very serious warning against the stage hypnotist practising their theatrical career and then setting themselves up as a hypnotherapist without training. Unfortunately many stage hypnotists have done exactly this and some even still practise stage hypnosis under a different name while running a hypnotherapy practice at the same time. Those stage hypnotists may also belong to what appears to be a recognised therapeutic organisation and there have been situations where some of these organisations have simply turned a blind eye to these activities.

The all-powerful stage hypnotist

McGill's book teaches the stage hypnotist to set themselves up in business and to frame their personality to the public as an all-powerful hypnotist. Although McGill tells the would-be hypnotist to make the subjects the stars of the show, the persona he encourages the stage hypnotist to adopt is one of authoritarianism. He tells the stage hypnotist to make the volunteers' hypnotic abilities the highlights of the performance, but in the same instance encourages the creation of a hypnotist who gets top billing.

As I command, so you will do!

This is the impression that the viewing public gets from such shows. The people sitting in the audience believe that the stage hypnotist possesses an ability to manipulate people against their will. It is one of the major principles that the stage hypnotist trades on. After all if all these wonderful volunteers were able to perform the unusual behaviours on their own, why would anyone need the stage hypnotist at all?

These are the kind of theatrical acts that, over the years, have included magic and conjuring tricks in order to bedazzle and amuse the public. In fact many magicians may have had some kind of training in hypnosis, using that ability to put over their tricks.

From a technical point of view, the stage hypnotist purports only to encourage the volunteer to do what comes naturally. They say that their volunteers are all exhibitionists, who have just been waiting for an opportunity to perform and that the job of the stage hypnotist is to bring them out of themselves. My observations have found this far from correct, as many of the badly damaged people I interviewed could have been decribed as quiet and introverted.

I met an elderly couple who had found themselves hypnotised by a magician at a children's school party. They were very angry because this had been done without their prior permission and they felt violated. When they found themselves seemingly stuck to the floor and unable to move, they became very upset and believed they were unable to do anything about it .

Of course there are many groups of individuals who think that hypnosis is an evil practice. Their understanding is that it is interfering with nature or the will of man or God; these people usually have a supply of quotes from prophets and soothsayers to support their ideas. They may see hypnosis as giving over a person's will unto another (Seventh Day Adventists) or going beyond the bounds of permissible interpersonal contact according to their belief systems.

Inevitably such viewpoints on human behaviour are nearly always tied up with religious mania, folk law and the rejection of scientific knowledge or empirical studies. It is unlikely they will have any knowledge of medicine, psychology, psychiatry or psychotherapy and they may also have beliefs that cite other forms of human behaviour as evil too.

The truth is though that they are not solely responsible for their perception of hypnosis, because over the years many stage hypnotists have billed themselves as being in possession of mystical powers. Such powers are often seen by the onlooker with fear, misunderstanding and a desire to banish these unexplained phenomena from their culture because they appear threatening.

If we look at a vast country like America, we can see how social order has had to be kept by many isolated and small communities. Each of them may have brought customs and beliefs of their own from the old world. To be confronted by different beliefs can be traumatic enough for cultures trying to preserve their roots, but to be faced with an apparently mystical power that appears to have the ability to dominate can be terrifying.

The English stage hypnotist, Paul McKenna, also purveyed the image of magical powers in his television show presented to the British public. A hypnotic induction is not allowed to be broadcast because it may accidentally induce trance in a person listening to or viewing that transmission. However, the editing of McKenna's shows went beyond deleting only the induction.

This clever editing of what may have been a two-hour show, down to 30 or 60 minutes of video tape, gave the impression to the public that hypnosis was an almost instant phenomenon. Few of the mechanics of the whole process were shown, leading the public to believe in McKenna's apparently magical ability to perform behavioural miracles.

People were instructed to carry out all sorts of ridiculous routines in order to amuse the audience. These volunteers were selected for their exceptionally suggestive personalities, so that McKenna would seem to have the most amazing power in controlling their behaviour. Many British professional hypnotherapists were very angry about this kind of public use of hypnosis that went out to millions of television viewers. They found that a lot of people who were presenting themselves for hypnotherapy were actually terrified of what might be done to them. Many had seen McKenna's show and had developed the belief that hypnosis was a tool with which one person could dominate another and make them do absolutely anything they wanted.

Educating the public

McKenna claimed to have brought hypnosis to millions of people who would not have considered it before. The consensus of the majority of people in the hypnotherapy profession was that hypnosis had been seen in a very bad light. Moreover many believe stage hypnosis should be banned for the safety of the public (See Chapter 8: The View of the Experts).

In 1996 a posting was placed on the internet, by Mark Casey, a hypnotherapist, commenting on how the popular resurgence of stage hypnosis on television seemed to have damaged the prospects of his business. Richard Bandler, the American hypnotist, replied to the posting, saying that if a therapist had not been getting the clients then they should look to their marketing.

It seems that Bandler did not appear to comprehend that we are not all international hypnotic celebrities, such as himself. Some therapists work in quiet backwaters where the influences of the media can make or break the public trust factor in hypnosis.

The travelling stage hypnotist is not an academic, nor a benevolent healer, so when they arrive in an alien environment they are perceived as a foreigner and such people are naturally viewed with suspicion. In a world of ever decreasing size, through the wonderful modern age of communication, life is often depicted as a homogeneous, interrelated cultural experience. But this is not as simple as it first appears because television, newspapers, and particularly governments are now viewed with just as much suspicion as they always were. It would, perhaps, even be true to say that authority is viewed with maybe even more suspicion than ever and this is now the way the authoritarian stage hypnotist is often seen.

Stage hypnotists seek to present the idea that it has been and still is stage hypnosis that educates the public to what is possible through hypnosis. They choose to ignore the history of hypnosis, denying that classical forms of hypnosis through hypnotherapy, medicine, healing, shamanism, dentistry, psychotherapy, education and religion existed long before stage hypnosis took its present form.

In the preface of *The New Encyclopedia of Stage Hypnotism*, McGill states that he hopes the medical profession will take hypnosis more seriously now and use it in place of drug therapy. What he ignores is that the medical and healing professions have often taken hypnosis very seriously indeed, but what they reject is its use as a source of entertainment.

There have been times when the healing professions have used hypnosis less, because of a shift in cultural, sociological or political perspectives. Nevertheless it would not be fair to say that hypnosis has been left in the care of stage hypnotists for its survival. Such ideas are based on illusions created by the stage hypnotists themselves and not historical fact.

Sensationalism

Sensibly McGill warns the stage hypnotist against playing for cheap laughs, although in an ever competitive world, this is advice that all stage hypnotists blatantly ignore. It seems that a headline in a Sunday tabloid is much more advantageous to a stage hypnotist's career than a commendable paragraph in *The Stage* or *Variety*.

Always looking for acts to pack in the audiences a theatrical agent will go for sensationalism every time. It was Malcolm McLaren, the manager of the punk band the Sex Pistols, in the 1970s who said: "Any publicity is good publicity." Let us also not forget how the American artist Andy Warhol made himself even more famous by filming heroin addicts and a plethora of people he considered to be down on their luck. From a publicist's standpoint all news is good news, no matter what it is, and no news is bad news. Sadly one controversial headline concerning a person who may have suffered side effects of stage hypnosis may rocket that hypnotist's bookings as opposed to dampening them.

Lawsuits

McGill's book even advises the would-be stage hypnotist

how to avoid lawsuits, but ignores the myriad of literature that has documented the large amount of knowledge about the side effects some people suffer after shows. Today's stage hypnotists are often able to circumnavigate the repercussions of a lawsuit, as they may have insurance policies that will pay out on legal costs and damages.

If damaged subjects were ever to receive a letter from a hypnotist's lawyer, threatening to counter sue them, they would more than likely feel very intimidated. The kind of person who volunteers for a stage hypnosis show is very suggestible and may be hypersensitive to threats. Also, the average person does not want to be involved in a lawsuit that may endanger their home, family and savings.

Bringing such an action in a court of law is an excruciatingly costly business and the complainant may not be able to afford the high legal costs that are involved. The stage hypnotist is, however, likely to be insured against such actions and all their legal costs catered for. Should the plaintiff commence the lawsuit and then not be able to proceed through lack of funds they will still be landed with large legal bills claimed from the defendant. In other words, the odds are greatly stacked against the volunteer to begin with, before they even start to try and prove their case.

In such a case the stage hypnotist will have rehearsed their reactions to any accusations of damage by reckless hypnosis, and they already know how to control their victim's emotions. The volunteer, however, is thrust into a world of confusion and becomes afraid. After all what do they know about hypnosis and how would they be able to find a lawyer who can even begin to understand what they were talking about?

There will be no body of tangible evidence for a judge to see and they will be unlikely to know anything about hypnosis either. The stage hypnotist knows how to present themselves confidently and is able to influence people with expertise. Let us not forget it is their job to influence people; this is what they do for a living. It is possible the stage hypnotist will use hypnosis to influence a judge and may choose a barrister who has had some training in hypnosis. I met one such barrister who had done a course, not only in hypnosis, but also acting and mime. This was quite a legitimate thing for him to be doing as his job was to plead his client's case. He said that whatever interpersonal skills he needed to argue a case, were not only legal, but were his duty to acquire.

Experts to give testimony can be available to support the evidence given by stage hypnotists, should they appear in court accused of a malpractice. There are a few experts who will say stage hypnosis is not harmful. No matter what the field, there is a need for the professionals who will give evidence in court and be paid for that service. The number of hypnotherapists, psychologists, psychiatrists or medical doctors who would testify that stage hypnosis is not a risk to the volunteers is very small, but these people do exist.

Any judge who is considering damage that has allegedly been done to a volunteer through stage hypnosis has to consider all the evidence offered by all parties. Those parties each present their own case and the experts are usually called in even numbers by all sides, leaving a person uneducated about hypnosis to come to a just decision about the claim. One of the problems in assessing the side effects of stage hypnosis often arises when psychologists, psychiatrists and medical doctors are called in.

Unfortunately the majority of these professionals have very little or no knowledge of hypnosis and its effects. They often end up giving opinions that miss all the relevant points about the hypnotic effects involved. Being trained in any of those professions does not necessarily qualify a person to know about hypnotic matters. However, I have found some of these professionals who have attempted to practise hypnosis badly. Only experts in hypnosis itself should be consulted when considering hypnotic effects.

The hypnotherapy profession

Another problem is the hypnotherapists themselves, who claim to be the world's best communicators and yet who seldom form into one main professional body to be consulted. In fact hypnotherapy is one of the most diverse professions with an endless plethora of different associations. This is because there are many different approaches within hypnotherapy, as hypnosis is used for a number of separate applications within medicine, dentistry, behavioural medicine, psychotherapy, counselling and even education.

There is often criticism from governments and the medical profession because hypnotherapy does not co-ordinate itself together in the manner that general medicine does, making it hard to consult as a profession, and this is very true. The stage hypnotist also relies on this diversity if they are ever caught up in a possible lawsuit.

Apart from the medical and dental uses of hypnosis, hypnotherapists use their own forms of psychotherapy to perform hypnotherapy. Within hypnotherapy there are the Freudians, Ericksonsions, Neuro-Linguistic-Programmers and traditional Direct Approach hypnotherapists. Each of these subgroups believes that their approach to hypnotherapy is the correct one. The stage hypnotist thrives on such inconsistency, knowing that they can virtually get away with anything while the hypnotherapists fight among themselves.

2

Hypnosis and Trance

What is trance ?

Trance can be said to be a state of being, induced by a state of mind. It is often described as an altered state of awareness, where the conscious critical mind steps out of the main focus, and allows an individual to operate through unconscious processes.

As we live, breathe, think and do, there are many processes happening within us and each of these are operated by different parts of us. We are higher life forms and need to have an incredibly complex amount of different things happening at the same time. Our main focus on the world, our window to the outside, is our consciousness. It is the part of us that makes contact with the world beyond our own bodies, helping us act into and react to the world.

Our unconscious is the rest of the processes that are running the remainder of the human experience, involuntarily and out of conscious awareness. Our blood, sugar levels, hormones, skin, memories and millions of internal mental patterns are being constantly monitored and activated by our infinitesimal amount of unconscious mechanisms.

Consciousness and voluntary experience is such a small part of the whole event, being less than 0.1%, and the unconscious remaining 99.9% or so is under the control of our unconscious. To some this may sound extreme and that is understandable when we consider how the West is obsessed with consciousness, denying that so much naturally remains unconscious.

Freud likened the unconscious mind to a huge iceberg that remains mostly under the water and the conscious mind to just the tip that sticks its head above. He took this idea from the early German romanticists but failed to understand its interpretation when he developed psycho-analysis. In psychoanalysis cure is sought by attempting to bring a person's memories of their life into their con-scious mind, but it ignored the fact that considering the proportions this would be mathematically impossible.

Trance is a state between wakefulness and sleep, a kind of unconsciousness where a person still retains some degree of contact with the outside world. This contact is different from the sleep or normal waking state because it is a process of selective attentiveness.

The word "trance" has a place in our common language; for example when someone is not paying attention they may be asked if they are in a trance. In the 1990s a resur-gence of trance dancing occurred where the person liter-ately dances themselves into a state of disassociated euphoria, sometimes under the influence of psychedelic or dance drugs, such as LSD or Ecstasy.

A person in a trance appears to be paying less attention to the external world (restricting reality testing), and they are in a partially or wholly disassociated state. They are, to a degree, *in absentea* of full consciousness.

Dr Milton Erickson, the American psychiatrist and hyp-notherapist, liked to define trance as a disassociated state where the individual is under the control of the uncon-scious processes (Rossi (ed) 1989 Vol 1). Wolinsky (1991), another hypnotherapist, believes that we are always in dif-ferent trances of varying kinds; to him they are like pat-terns of behaviours. He considers that the job of a hypnotherapist is to break the old trance and help the person install a new one that will serve a desired purpose.

To the stage hypnotist trance is the state that has been induced in the volunteers, and is under the hypnotist's control. The stage hypnotist is an entertainer who needs to be seen as the most important element in the show. Hypnosis and trance are the commodities that the stage hypnotist wants the public to believe that they bring to the show; it is what the hypnotist is selling. They need to appear to control those commodities in order for their act to be re-booked.

Your trance will develop and it will be your own individual experience, but you will do everything I say

There has been much investigation over the years as to whether the state of trance really does exist. Each time a person who is intellectually unfamiliar with the trance state, encounters it they carry out an internal debate in order to make sense of it. For my investigations in this book I shall be presupposing that trance does exist, both as a special state of being and as a series of multiple patterns of behaviours.

What is hypnosis?

Hypnosis is the induction of the altered state of trance. It may be auto-hypnosis (self-hypnosis) or hetero-hypnosis (being taken into trance by another person). Among hypnotists there is a common belief that all hypnosis is a form of self-hypnosis, in that a person may not be induced into trance if they do not want to be and no one can impose trance upon another. This is really a metaphor constructed to bypass the subject's conscious defence mechanisms and the professionals' protection against any lawsuit. If the hypnotist claims that the subject hypnotised themselves, then there would never be a case for malpractice, since the hypnotist disclaims responsibility.

During auto-hypnosis a person makes suggestions to themselves to narrow down and restrict their attention to the outside world (restricting reality testing), and to pay attention to their internal mental processes. We live in a world that is so obsessed with measuring our experiences against the competitive levels of others that we often forget the rich world of imagination that exists within us all.

Our minds are the drivers of our bodies, which are the vehicles in which we travel through our human existence. All action, reaction, function, dysfunction, inception of being and emotionality comes about through the initiation of cognitive processes. To induce in ourselves a state of trance through self-suggestion is to pay attention to ourselves, thoughts, mental processes and allow the seeds of imagination to ignite new experience. I remember when training as a hypnotherapist my tutor saying: "If you want to be a hypnotist, first you can imagine you are a hypnotist in your own mind."

When people discover how to induce trance in themselves, through self-hypnosis, they can find it an incredibly liberating experience. There is a sense of being given back control of your own mind, breaking with the pressuring influences of the outside world and becoming the captain of your own ship.

In the therapeutic situation it is useful for the client to consider that all hypnosis is actually self-hypnosis. People come to therapists with problems, often feeling unhappy, frightened and with a sense that they are no longer in control of their lives, selves or behaviours. The last thing they need is an oppressive, self-opinionated, authoritarian commanding them, because that may simply cause them to reject any helpful suggestions that may be offered.

So the hypnotherapist seeks to gain a sense of rapport and part of that rapport can be to metaphorically hand over control of the trance experience to the client by implying that all hypnosis is self-hypnosis. It is also a way of empowering and boosting the ego of the client, who is often at a low ebb about their perceived dysfunction. The therapist further seeks to teach their client to be less dependent on the therapist and instead to be autonomous by becoming their own self-hypnotist. Consequently the client can perceive any progress that happens in therapy as being a result of their own resources.

In hetero-hypnosis the hypnotist guides the subject into a state of trance, and one of the most amazing things is that generally when a person goes into a deep trance they become more suggestible. However, people do not realise that they are also very suggestible when they are in the waking state too and this is how the hypnotist gets them into trance in the first place.

So is all hypnosis self-hypnosis?

The answer to that would have to be no. We are simply passing from one trance to the next in our varying levels of consciousness.

We can attempt to view the hypnotic process as being an interaction between the hypnotist and those hypnotised. Just like table tennis there are at least two players required. The game may be supported by one player being compensatory for the other's lack of experience, but it still requires all parties to be participants, or else there is no game.

We are hypnotised every day by everyone we meet and by all of the incoming information that we are receiving. Our narrowing of attention to a particular stream of incoming information makes us susceptible to any suggestion that it may contain. To a certain degree, everyone is constantly hypnotising everyone else.

A hypnotist has been trained to spot the kind of signs that indicate a person is ready to move to the next altered state of consciousness. The hypnotist then utilises suggestion techniques to direct the subject's unconscious.

In order to process a suggestion the subject must first consume the information, turn it into a thought, which then stands a chance of becoming an action. If the suggestion is rejected by the subject a hypnotist simply makes another suggestion until they reach one that incites the desired effect.

Human beings are so complex that the dynamics that are taking place at all levels of consciousness during hypnosis are both active and reactive. Logically it cannot be said therefore, that the hypnosis is solely the responsibility of either the hypnotist or the subject. Both parties are participating in the procedure at an unconscious level; however, the subject may be operating without conscious awareness, while the hypnotist is consciously aware of what is happening.

The implications of this are that the subjects of stage hypnosis may be operating without their conscious critical defence mechanisms being in tact, thereby rendering them vulnerable to the will of the hypnotist. If the presupposition exists that the stage hypnotist has their subject's health and welfare as the main priority, all well and good, but their primary goal is to be entertaining.

The professional hypnotist is an expert in human communications, who uses not only words to deliver their suggestions, but also voice tones, body language, visual cues, touch and even third parties. The majority of communications between people take place on an unconscious level and only the tip of the communication is recognised by the conscious mind. A hypnotist knows how to form a communication so it can bypass a person's conscious critical awareness and implant suggestion directly into the unconscious.

This is a skill, craft, art, science, knowledge and ability that the hypnotist has systematically learnt and not some kind of mysterious, mystical gift.

There can be no static or solid definition of what hypnosis is exactly, for every hypnotic situation is different and each hypnotic interaction contains its own exclusive dynamics.

Can trance and hypnosis exist separately?

Since trance can be a naturally occurring process that happens spontaneously, it arises nearly all the time without hypnosis eg watching television, reading, memory recall, driving a car along the motorway without paying conscious attention to the mechanics of the driving, contemplation and attending to internal cognitive processing.

The use of hypnosis as a tool to induce trance can be carried out as part of the normal unconscious communication mechanisms between people or through the inducer's conscious attention. The parties involved in that hypnotic process may be more than one individual or more than one parts of the psyche, in the case of self-hypnosis.

*As you go into trance you will find it impossible to resist
my suggestions*

During the show you will obey my commands

Hypnosis is a communication mechanism, therefore it is
apart from trance in that it is an action, not a state. To be
engaged hypnotically does not necessarily mean that an
overtly identified state of trance will occur. During the
hypnotic encounter the trance state can appear invisible
to the conscious mind.

*You may think you are awake...you may have your eyes
open... but you are in a trance*

To all hypnotists this invisibility can be important
because it means they can have people hypnotised, in
trance, without that person being consciously aware of
what is happening. For the clinician this is seen as a therapeutic technique; for the stage hypnotist it is perceived as
a sleight of hand.

What is the placebo effect?

The placebo effect is an effective way of turning
thoughts into actions and widely used in all forms of medicine, psychology, therapy and social control. The belief
that something will happen is often quite sufficient, in
some cases, to cause an effect. People are generally con-
strained by sociocultural constructed beliefs that prohibit
them from turning many thoughts into actions.

There can also be personal psychological constructs
that people have built up in their minds, which can cause
them not to believe that something can happen. Often
what is needed is for them just to be told, either consciously or unconsciously, that something can happen
and this cause will bring about an effect.

People get better from illnesses everyday by simply

being told they will get better by doctors and nurses. Educators induce states of intellectual competence in students by telling them they have the capabilities to complete their studies. Drug trials test the effectiveness of medicine by giving some control subjects the real drug and some a dummy one. Strangely enough a lot of the people taking the dummy medication get better too because they believe they are consuming the real medicine. The power of the mind over matter is far stronger than the philosophies and politics of our times purvey.

There have been many theorists who have tried to put forward the idea that hypnosis and trance are simply the results of the placebo effect. The hypnotist tells the person they will go into trance and they go into trance. While there are always large elements of the placebo effect in the hypnotic relationship, it cannot be held solely responsible for the effects of hypnosis.

In stage hypnosis, if the placebo effect is identified as being the sole contingent of hypnosis, then there could not be a case to ban it, because it would be identified as little more than mere suggestion.

Expectancy precedes trance

This is the precursor to the placebo effect, since it is not necessarily linear to hypnosis, but a preceding set of beliefs: an anticipation that something will happen arises. Hypnotists use expectancy all the time by seeding ideas, through suggestion, in order to create the right mind set needed to then initiate hypnosis.

The volunteer in the stage hypnosis show has brought with them much expectancy to the performance. They expected to see a performance of stage hypnosis; expected to see someone hypnotised; expected to partake in the stage hypnosis show when they were chosen as a volunteer; expected to be hypnotised; and expected to automatically comply involuntarily to the hypnotist's suggestions.

As part of pacing their possible future events people are always in a state of expectation about themselves, others and situations. Stage hypnosis volunteers have brought with them their own expectations to play the role of the hypnotic subject. The hypnotist then adds to those expectations, via suggestion, during the preliminary audience hypnosis. There is also a large amount of audience expectation in the context of stage hypnosis, which compounds the equation. The audience expects someone to be hypnotised, so the volunteers attempt to fulfil that role.

Some volunteers expect to have a good time and do. Unfortunately some expect to be dominated, controlled, made to perform ridiculous tasks and for something to go wrong, so it does. The minimal time and attention paid to each individual during the process of stage hypnosis prevents the stage hypnotist checking whether the expectations of the volunteers are healthy enough to anticipate a good outcome.

I know you are all excited about the show

Excitement is also a very pertinent part of the stage hypnosis scenario that adds to the formulation of the show and performance of the subjects. Everyone at the show has an outpouring of energy, which must inevitably be directed towards a goal. The stage hypnotist understands this equation and utilises the free flow of energy to direct the audience and subjects alike towards creating the hypnotic show in accordance with the expectations that are running high.

MODELS OF HYPNOSIS

The expansionist model
For our considerations of what stage hypnosis might or might not be, it is essential to look at the boundaries that define hypnosis as a whole. The expansionist concept of hypnosis is one held by those who perceive hypnosis to incorporate all forms of interpersonal relationships, where one person makes a suggestion and another person responds to those suggestions. In hetero-hypnosis that

would be the hypnotist and the subject, and in self-hypnosis it would be the communication between the different aspects of the psyche.

This would logically incorporate waking suggestion. To the lay person this may not seem to be hypnosis at all, but according to this model, it is. The expansionists believe that the very relationship which is taking place is, in fact, hypnotic in itself. One element is entrancing another (focusing attention) and then delivering a communication that contains a suggestion. In entertainment hypnosis the expansionist state of waking suggestion is the first of the three part process: waking trance, sleeping trance and artificial somnambulism (See chapter three: Inductions and Suggestions).

From the expansionist point of view a progressive continuum of the hypnotic relationship does not depend on the traditional representation of hypnosis, where the subject appears to be asleep. Neither does it hold the belief that relaxation is necessary as a precursor to including a trance-like state.

In this book I have applied the expansionist concept to the actions of stage hypnosis, since I am identifying the whole relationship between the subject and the stage hypnotist as being hypnotic. Therefore all three states involved in stage hypnosis, as mentioned above, are covered by the expansionist spectrum. I realise that there is a danger here that an argument could be put forward proposing that hypnosis then is not a special relationship, since it might be viewed simply as part of interpersonal relationships as a whole.

The reductionist model
This is the perception of hypnosis as a special state, and one which would comply more to the traditional image of the hypnotic relationship, where there is a dominant person who induces sleep and an obedient state in another. This has become less popular in recent years, but is certainly still the main formula of stage hypnosis, where a controller is seen to be the sole initiator of behaviours in

the subject.

There have been studies that have argued that suggestion is heightened in this reductionist state and refer to waking suggestion as being non-hypnotic. From the position of the experimental hypnotist, who works mainly in a laboratory and generally under artificial conditions, it is essential to have an identified commodity to quantify and investigate. Such experimentalists, whose agendas are research, have enormous problems in coming to terms with the expansionist model of hypnosis because it always challenges the validity of their research.

However, it is useful, at times, to present to the hypnotic subject a concept of reductionist hypnosis in order to utilise the placebo effect. In the clinical context hypnotherapists use the illusion of reductionist hypnosis while also working with the clients' unconscious processes out of conscious awareness, on an expansionist basis.

From a modular point of view, in stage hypnosis the reductionist elements are the second and third states of trance.

Is trance a form of sleep?

This must depend on the form of trance and hypnosis being used. Hypnotists over the years have put forward this idea in order to retain hypnosis as a special skill and trance as a special state. Clinical hypnotists, according to whether they are expansionists or reductionists, will or will not, associate trance with a sleep-like state. There are times when it is psychologically beneficial to the subject to believe that trance is a form of sleep.

The stage hypnotist trades very heavily upon the idea, in the audiences mind, that hypnosis is preceded by the sleep-like induction. The hypnotist wants the audience to believe that when the subject is under hypnosis, they are controlled in that sleep-like state. The audience sees the hypnotist using the cue word SLEEP and then suddenly the subject appears asleep. It is empowering to the stage hypnotist's image to have it believed that they are controlling people by sending them to sleep and then telling them what to do.

> *You will sleep and when you wake up*
> *you will do as I say*

But hypnosis is not sleep; it is a state of physiological and mental being that can sometimes be between the states of wakefulness and sleep. The reductionists would argue that trance can only exist between these two states, but the expansionists would argue that trance can also exist in the state of wakefulness too.

There have been studies that have tried to measure whether suggestions delivered in the waking conscious-ness are as effective as the ones delivered in the state of the traditional, sleep associated, trance-like states. Such studies must depend entirely on being carried out under artificial circumstances, for there is always the element of transference from the experimenter to the subject and the experiment itself will corrupt the study.

Many hypnotists believe that it is only in the sleep asso-ciated states that suggestions are delivered effectively and that suggestions delivered in wakefulness are less effec-tive. However, the cognitive behavioural elements of any interpersonal relationship are bound to affect the person involved in that relationship, who is receiving the sugges-tions. In other words, as far as a stage hypnotist is con-cerned, even though they lead the audience to believe that hypnosis is preceded by sleep, this is not the case because they are working with the first state of stage hypnosis, the waking trance.

The expansionist view of waking hypnosis
To call this hypnosis at all is a challenge to our society's traditional view of the stupefied, and obedient hypnotic subject. Many behaviourists would hotly contest that it is not hypnosis, but merely responsiveness to waking sug-gestion. Trance has been defined as being the state that occurs when the brain moves out of beta and high beta

wave activity, down to alpha, theta and even delta. Beta and high beta are the normal waking states and the neo-cortical activity diminishes as the person passes down through alpha and theta until the subject is fully asleep in the delta state. For the reductionist all hypnosis and trance must be classified as taking place in that alpha state or below.

However, the expansionist recognises that hypnotic interpersonal relationships also take place when people are in the beta and high beta states. By looking at crowd control the expansionist's viewpoint can be confirmed. In a riot people are in a state of excitation and high beta wave brain wave activity; however, they can also be so focused that they are unaware of their wider surroundings, devoid of what is going on around them. Their attention has narrowed and they have reduced reality testing. Although they are in states of extreme wakefulness, they may also be in a trance.

If we look sociologically at the influences of leaders from Moses through to Napoleon, Hitler and all the way to Billy Graham, we can see that a hypnotic influence is taking place. The waking state of trance is used to narrow the focus of attention of the masses, to reduce reality testing and to implant suggestion.

In stage hypnosis the hypnotist is not only hypnotising the volunteers but the audience too. While they use hypnosis to produce the three states of trance with the volunteers, they generally only need to use the first state of waking hypnosis with the audience.

What also happens is that several members of the audience actually go into the third, deeper state of artificial somnambulism during the show, some going from the first state of waking trance directly to artificial somnambulism, missing out the second sleeping state.

And some of you in the audience may even go into trance

Let us remember as well, that all hypnotists are word-smiths and illusionists; these are the tools of our trade, the magic with which we weave spells, and the hidden medicine with which we heal.

THEORIES OF HYPNOSIS

Neo-dissasociation theory

The neo-disassociation theory was made popular by Hilgard (1994) of Stanford University. This is not like the old disassociation theory whereby a process that is out of control of consciousness can be interpreted as having a pathological base. Hilgard proposes that consciousness is composed of many levels of the psyche, some of which are in conscious awareness and some of which are not.

The cognitive processes (thoughts actions), that are in conscious awareness, are carried out with intention, voluntarily. The processes that are carried on out of conscious awareness are automatic, involuntary and not under the control of conscious intention. Since conscious awareness is seen as only a tiny part of the whole of thought mechanisms, it would be logical that Hilgard regards most of our thought mechanisms to be unconscious.

We have many levels of awareness, each of which we can label as a state. The state that is occupying consciousness is said to be fulfilling the role of the executive ego. Since consciousness is a small space, only one state can occupy the executive function at one time; all the other states, or levels of processing remain unconscious and carry out their functions automatically eg the knee jerk reaction, blushing, sexual attraction, phobias, habits, some actions and all reactive behaviours.

Hilgard believes that we are associated to the state that is in the position of the executive ego and the rest are floating around in a disassociative manner. Those that carry on their processes automatically, from a disassociated position, do not have any conscious intent in what they do.

In hypnosis Hilgard thinks that the conscious awareness is put to one side and that the person functions in one or more of those disassociated unconscious states. The focus of attention changes to a disassociated state, therefore there can be a lack of awareness consciously. One state may not be aware of another's functions, sometimes causing amnesia about what is happening, whether naturally or as a result of suggestion.

The conscious mind's job seems to be to focus attention on a narrow stream of thoughts which fulfil the need of the moment. When that need has passed, the focus of attention changes as another state moves into conscious awareness, demanding attention.

Psychoanalytical theory

Freud's model of the human mind was rooted firmly in the conception of behaviour being grounded in childhood and the person being subject to those patterns for the rest of their lives. Psychoanalysts (Fromm 1979) see hypnosis as a form of regression to being in the childlike, sublimated state.

There is also the concept that the subject, in hypnosis, is falling under the dominance and sexual libido of the hypnotist. To the non-Freudian this may seem extraordinarily obsessive with sexual behaviours, but to the paradigm of psychoanalysis, this is a logical extension of their philosophies.

Bearing in mind that in his early days Freud worked dissecting brains, he added to his notions that hypnosis was also a physiological evolutionary regression. Freudians believe that in hypnosis a person is abandoning some of the higher newly acquired intellectual processes and reverting to primary behaviours.

Freud abandoned hypnosis very early on, believing it to be of little use, but the reason was actually because he was not a very good hypnotist. He also studied in Paris, at the Salpêtrière with Charcot, whose associations between hypnotic ability and mental dysfunction eventually became widely discredited and rejected.

Social psychological theory

This has been investigated by Spanos (1986) and Wagstaff

(1979), both of whom have published many papers on their criticism of the neo-dissasociaton theory of hypnosis and their support of the theory of social compliance: we each act in accordance with the people around us, complying to social rules, personal dynamics, undeclared intentions, expectations, prohibitions and hidden agendas.

The social psychologists work mainly with the view that conscious intent is always part of the hypnotic behaviour, therefore it is not an unconscious process and there can be no such thing as hypnosis. It is a terrible dilemma they put themselves in, for having identified hypnosis, they then say there can be no such thing. It is undoubtedly throwing the baby out with the bath water.

This can dangerously make them an ally to the stage hypnotists because they are the perfect kind of expert witness to contest the existence of hypnosis. Without hypnosis a stage hypnotist cannot be sued for harming anyone with it. There seems to be a disturbing denial of experience here in the effort to prove a theory.

Is hypnosis pretending or is pretending hypnosis?

Is a person really hypnotised in the stage show or are they just playing along with the expectations of the hypnotist, the audience, or themselves?

If they are just playing along could this mean there is no possibility of being damaged?

From the expansionist point of view, even when someone is pretending to be hypnotised, they are hypnotised, because they are altering their cognitive processes in accordance with the instruction of the hypnotist. This can be so, even though the volunteer may have hidden agendas that prevent them from co-operating wholly in the experience. If they break out of that trance at any time during the show, they have still complied and at some level reacted to the hypnotist's suggestions.

In their selection procedures the stage hypnotist tries to filter out those who have the hidden agenda of only pretending to be hypnotised by using the following suggestion at the beginning of the show.

I only want those people who genuinely want to be hypnotised to come up on the stage.

Because if you want to challenge me to hypnotise you against your will, it won't happen and you will be wasting your time.

So only those who genuinely have a desire to be hypnotised during the show can be among the volunteers.

Inevitably those who have come up to the stage with hidden agendas will give an indication of this through their behaviour and reactions, and the stage hypnotist will simply ask them to sit back in the audience and enjoy the show. After all no performer wants unco-operative props. The stage hypnotist may send a volunteer back to their seat at any time of the show, thereby getting rid of anyone who may have the malicious intention of being a trickster and ruining their show.

Early into the show the stage hypnotist can very easily spot those who are not demonstrating genuine hypnotic phenomena. There are, of course, those who come out of trance during the show and rather than hypnotise them again the hypnotist usually asks them to return to their seats.

From the social compliance point of view no one has been genuinely hypnotised and therefore cannot have been damaged by the experience. From the expansionist perceptive all participants are in hypnotic compliance and the volunteer may be damaged.

Skeleton key theory

Barber (Lynn, Rhue 1991) talks about his analogy of the locksmith's model applied to hypnosis. This is the concept that the hypnotist is tinkering around with a skeletal key, until a series of unconscious locks are turned. While primarily it may sound imprecise, it is, in fact, a very clear understanding of what a hypnotist does. The hypnotist has experience in knowing which mental and physical barrels to turn, buttons to push, reactions to elicit and psychological locks to pick.

On a very limited basis, a stage hypnotist may easily learn some procedures that can elicit hypnotic phenomena sufficiently to construct a show for entertainment purposes. However, it is unlikely that they will have any training in therapy or psychological theories. Therefore, having created a state of deep trance in a subject, through hypnosis, they are unlikely to understand what some of the consequences of their actions could be.

Could a person who can open a lock with a hammer be considered a skilled locksmith?

Or could someone with a carving knife who can dig out an appendix be considered a surgeon?

The ecosystemic theory

The interconnectedness of everything is the way Fourie (1989) chooses to consider the trance experience and the hypnotic process. This line of thinking does not take on the either/or debate of state or non-state hypnosis, but perceives that there is an infinitesimal amount of combined variables playing out the scenario.

There is a realisation that in order to study a phenomenon it does, at times, need to be reduced to something scientifically quantifiable, but then to judge it that way induces distortion. Here the Heisenberg Uncertainty Principle must apply, in that the results of a study are dependent upon the questions that are asked, the place they are asked from, and are only a representation of that observation. Should the results of that study then be generalised to apply to the whole of a phenomenon, a distorted truth occurs.

Theories of hypnosis were sought in order to dispel the mystical misconceptions of hypnosis; however, if each set of ideas are considered in isolation, they cannot apply to the whole. In other words, experts on hypnosis tend to hold a certain set of ideas according to their observations and there is no single theory of hypnosis that can apply to the whole phenomenon.

If an expert witness appears in court to give information to a judge concerning damage caused by a hypnotist, it is perfectly possible for that witness to be chosen for their particular view of hypnosis. However, the judge is in danger of believing that the expert witness may be offering the view on hypnosis *per se* and as we have seen, there is no one core model which is available to use at the moment. In fact, because hypnosis covers such a huge amount of considerable eventualities, it is unlikely that there ever will be a central theory, only a dispersement of observations.

The social-psychobiological theory

Banyai (Lynn & Rhue 1991) from Hungary has proposed a social, psychological and physiological theory of hypnosis, which takes in all the aforementioned elements and considers the neurological occurrences that take place during the process of hypnosis and in trance. She sees the hypnotic process as something that can be studied within the laboratory context, thereby disclosing knowledge about human interaction in general.

This can, in some way, be seen in contradiction to the more Ericksonian expansive, communication based considerations of hypnosis. Although Erickson wrote many papers on his experiments with hypnosis, which he conducted both in the laboratory and in the field, he viewed hypnosis, in later life, as something that was seen differently in the field than in the laboratory.

These considerations have great bearing on the way we

look at stage hypnosis, because while academic experimentalism may be used in some contexts as a measure for hypnotic responsiveness, it cannot apply to the field experience of stage hypnosis.

There are too many variables involved in the process of stage hypnosis for it to be studied anywhere but in the field. That is not to say that the victims who suffer side effects cannot be studied after the event, either clinically or experimentally, but it would be taking the experience out of context to study the process other than in the field.

Is it really important to study such small numbers of people who have been damaged?

Certainly it is true that stage hypnosis is a minuscule portion of the application of hypnosis and the amount of people who suffer severe damage from the process is very small. However, having said that, it does not make it less important than other aspects of hypnotic phenomena. In studying it, things become evident that reflect upon our understanding of human nature as a whole.

Learning what we ought not to do to each other is an important part of the process that defines what we can do to each other to help, dispel or alleviate human suffering and improve the lot of humanity as a whole. Perhaps, as I digress into philosophy, I can tell you I believe, as do the vast majority of those who use hypnosis, that its utilisation can immensely improve the human condition and it should not be used to harm.

Unfortunately there are those who have little regard for the safety of their hypnotic subjects. They are embarking upon a crusade to bolster their own egos as hypnotists and earn a great deal of money or prestige. It is not that there is anything wrong with a healer making a comfortable living out of the skills they have worked so hard to acquire; after all the dignity of the healer only adds to the dignity of the patient, but there needs to be limits.

A hypnotist who puts the expediency of showmanship or money above the well-being of the hypnotic subject may construct any theory they wish from the diverse observations made about hypnotic phenomena to defend their position, but it does not alter the fact that some people are damaged by stage hypnosis.

What is hypnosis and trance, therefore, is dependent upon the application, context, parties involved, philosophies, social constructs, ideologies, hypnotists, subjects and specific experiences.

To the public stage hypnosis is the induction of a special state induced by the stage hypnotist in the subject to compel that person to obey their commands. For the experimental hypnotist it can be any number of experiences according to the questions they ask, which are determined by their observational perspective. For the clinician, who uses hypnosis for healing, stage hypnosis is an abuse of an ability that disregards the well-being of the subjects. For the legislator it is a nightmare that defies classification, and the more experts they ask, the more ambiguous the answers become.

3

Inductions and Suggestions

One of the things that the stage hypnotist depends on is the fact that it is the most suggestible of people that actually go to hypnosis shows in the first place. From there the selection procedure filters down to the even more suggestible of that group, through a series of tests. An audience will be asked at the beginning of the show to help the hypnotist in an experiment. They will all be given a series of tasks and those who perform them to the stage hypnotist's satisfaction will be invited up on the stage as volunteers.

Selection procedures
This selection procedure may involve what is called the hand clasp test or the arm levitation test, and some stage hypnotists have their own individual suggestibility tests. In the hand clasp test it is suggested to the audience that they stand and then hold their arms and hands directly out in front of them. After they have clasped their hands together with interlocking fingers, it is then suggested that they use imaginary superglue or magnetism to bond them together so nothing can break them apart. Compounded suggestions are used to implant in the audience's minds the idea that the hands have become inseparable. Finally they are then challenged to see if they can take their hands apart and the ones that cannot do this are in the higher suggestibility group.

In the hand levitation test it is again suggested that the arms are held forward at the height of the chest. One hand is to face palm open upwards, and the other palm open downwards. With their eyes closed, the audience is invited to imagine that one arm has a balloon filled with helium tied to it and the other has a stone attached to it. Some of the audience will end up with one arm in the air and the other down by their sides; once again these are the suggestible type. People who may have passed both tests will be demonstrating their extreme suggestibility and are prime subjects for the stage hypnotist.

Cleverly the hypnotist makes these tests sound as if the people who demonstrate their extreme suggestibility have some kind of excellent hypnotic power. An audience is always happy to please a good entertainer, as they perceive it as adding to their own enjoyment of a show. The selected members of the audience, who then get invited on to the stage, are truly the most suggestible people present. The are referred to as the committee and are well suited to go through to the new round of selection procedures.

Screening procedures

As the volunteers are invited onto the stage some hypnotists ask people who are subject to epilepsy, depression or mental illness not to step forward, but some hypnotists make no such requests. This is the extent of the screening procedure that the stage hypnotist carries out. It is composed of a few sentences projected from the stage in a matter of no more then 10 seconds during a moment of audience excitement and confusion. In the consulting room the professional hypnotherapist will often spend more than 30 minutes or more collecting a case history or details of their client before attempting to use hypnosis.

Such a screening procedure is a statutory part of the client and therapist relationship that is demanded by all professional organisations. Its purpose is to screen for any people who have mental illnes or unforeseen circumstances that will make them contraindicated to hypnosis. Enough emphasis cannot be placed on the importance of this screening procedure that is used by professional clinicians who utilise hypnosis. It is important to acquire a large body of knowledge about a person before inducing profound hypnosis.

Some volunteers may be undiagnosed depressives, who may consider that the magic of the stage hypnotist has some powers or transformational properties on their inner feelings. There is the borderline personality who may be verging on the edge of mental illness but has not yet sought help, or people with minor neuroses, who have developed self-management strategies that could be undermined by the stage hypnosis experience.

Different states of trance in stage hypnosis

According to the kind of hypnosis that is taking place, different states of trance experience are identified. When discussing stage hypnosis I shall identify three such states:

1st state: hypnoidal or waking trance
2nd state: sleeping trance
3rd state: artificial somnambulism

Here I am considering stage hypnosis solely for entertainment, but when profiling other forms of hypnosis there may be a greater or lesser number of states to the trance experience.

Many of the subjects that have been invited onto the stage will already be in a state of waking trance. The expectation of being hypnotised by the powerful stage hypnotist will have sent these highly suggestive individuals into a state of trance already. They will have less awareness of their surroundings, having a narrowed field of focus and will appear to be gazing into space. The stage hypnotist will earmark those who demonstrate such behaviour.

Inductions

With their volunteers on the stage the hypnotist will now implement the next step of their selection procedure, the official induction of trance. To the audience it will appear that the stage hypnotist is now going to weave their magic spell, but in actual fact, the procedure of developing trance in those volunteers is already well underway.

The induction of a profound state of trance can be carried out in endless ways as there are literally thousands of classical inductions that a hypnotist may use to guide a subject into trance via hypnosis. Indeed the experienced hypnotist can simply devise a method of their own that will suit their purposes. What they are looking for are certain reactions in an individual to tell them that the subject has now entered the next stage of deeper trance. Having seen that reaction, the stage hypnotist then knows that this will be a responsive subject, who will be the kind of volunteer that they can rely on to entertain their audiences.

Some of the people who have been invited onto the stage and who do not demonstrate the kind of responses the stage hypnotist wants will be thanked and then politely asked to rejoin the audience and enjoy the show. The selection continues until the volunteers that are left are the kinds of highly suggestible people that the stage hypnotist can work with to their satisfaction.

Let us look very carefully here, and we can see how those extremely highly suggestible people come to be the chosen volunteers. Out of a town of 10,000 people, 500 of the most suggestible will come to the show. Then maybe 50 will indicate more suggestibility through the hand clasp, arm levitation or other selection experiments. Finally 10 people may be left on the stage as the chosen volunteers. In such a scenario they are the 0.1% who will guarantee to be very responsive to the stage hypnotist's suggestions. They will also have been chosen for their potential to enter the deepest state of trance, artificial somnambulism, also known as the awake-sleeping state of hypnosis.

A typical official trance induction will possibly include the eye rolling method, where the volunteers will be asked to roll their eyeballs backwards over the back of their heads until they feel they are underneath their eyelids. Remaining in this posture for some considerable time, sitting or standing, has the effect of sending some people into trance. When they are then asked to close their eyes and **GO TO SLEEP** they move into the second state of trance, the sleeping state.

Another induction is the handshake confusion technique, popularised by Erickson, who used it in demonstration hypnosis. In this technique the subject's attention is attracted and then confused by an unusual handshake. This handshake would be other than they may have expected, and the confusion then makes them susceptible to accepting the next suggestion that is offered to them. The hypnotist offers the suggestion that they **GO TO SLEEP** and in confusion they accept it.

This induction makes it appear to the onlooker that the effect is instant. The reality is that the subject is already deep in the first, hypnoidal, state of trance. Then the confusion of the unexpected nature of the handshake and instant suggestions simply slips the subject quickly into the second, sleeping state of trance. As the head falls forwards and the subject is subdued, it creates a very dramatic interpretation of the situation to the audience.

The falling induction is a classic one used by stage hypnotists and is often used in America by Evangelical preachers during religious meetings. As the hypnotist sees the individual moving deep into waking trance, they use one hand to support the volunteer's back and the other hand to suggest closure of eyes while the subject is falling backwards to the floor, being supported from behind. As they are falling a suggestion is made that they are falling into a deep trance and will sleep.

As the volunteers, one by one, pass from the first, waking state of trance, of which the audience is not aware, to the second, sleeping state of trance, the stage hypnotist is monitoring their subjects to check that they are responding to the suggestions.

One of the standard ways of deepening trances is to use the fractionation technique, where a subject is reawakened to perform a task and then afterwards put back into the second, sleeping state. This has the effect of deepening the trance and also gives a flow to the entertainment value of the show, making it appear as if the subject is beginning to come under the stage hypnotist's spell.

Somnambulists
Hypnotists often work with light states of trance and do

not generally take everyone into the deeper state of artificial somnambulism. Here it is also useful to distinguish between artificial somnambulism and instant somnambulism. Artificial somnambulism is the third state induced by taking the person through each of the previous two states.

Some of the audience will be what is called instant somnambulists, that is they will spontaneously go into trance at the very mention of hypnosis or will already be in a state of waking trance that the stage hypnotist can utilise. Such subjects are easy to spot to the trained eye and they will be looked for among the volunteers because their natural ability to be in a state of waking trance will save the stage hypnotist a great deal of work. If the performer is a well-known individual, playing to a large audience, they may employ their own specially trained security guards or minders, who will know what to look for in subjects and point those individuals out to the performer.

It is estimated that one in five people are natural somnambulists and are very good at going into deep levels of trance. These are the volunteers that the stage hypnotists wants. Despite misconceptions everyone is capable of going into deep states of trance, but some people take longer to train than others, and stage hypnotists want instant results, so they select their volunteers very carefully.

In contrast to the clinician it is important to the stage hypnotist that every subject on the stage appears to pass through the second, sleeping state of trance in order to become artificially somnambulistic. This creates the illusion that the stage hypnotist has the power to put people in and out of the second sleeping state by some mystical, magical power.

Progressive suggestions are made to the volunteers to descend deeper and deeper into a more relaxed state, becoming more and more entranced. At this point the stage hypnotist puts in a cue word or phrase to associate the subject with the second, sleeping stage of trance. The word or phrase is usually **SLEEP** or **GO TO SLEEP**.

The stage hypnotist suggests to the subjects that from now on, each time the cue **SLEEP** is used the volunteer will fall back into the second state of trance. Attached to this auditory anchor may also be a light touch on a shoulder to strengthen the suggestion across two of the five senses. Furthermore the stage hypnotist may also have a certain facial look associated to the cue, in order for the suggestion to be processed in three of the subject's sensory systems: sound, touch and sight.

Sleepers

It is important that the stage hypnotist is able to get the subject to react instantly to the suggestions and then at the command **SLEEP** to go back into the second, sleeping state of trance. When a sketch has run its course the stage hypnotist needs to be able to control the situation and move on to the next vignette.

Here it is wise to point out the difference between a person's susceptibility to go into trance and their suggestibility. While many people may have a susceptibility to go quickly into deep trance, this does not mean they will be any good as volunteers to the stage hypnotist. It is important to the stage show that the subject is primarily responsive to suggestion. A person who is solely susceptible to go into deep trance, but does not respond to suggestion, will be of little entertainment value and will become what can be called sleepers.

Sleepers can be dead weights to a stage hypnotist because they remain predominantly in the second state of trance, not responding to suggestions. They may fall off chairs, the stage or be unable to stand up. If they are not returned to their seats early in the show they are generally given a reactive task and made to sit in the same spot while the other volunteers are concentrated on. There may be an association word programmed into them which causes them to respond each time they hear a certain phrase, such as laughing at the word "chocolate". This way they keep their entertainment value but their inability to react to a wide range of suggestions is not noticed.

Artificial somnambulism

In order to set all this up so that the committee appears to be responding instantly to the stage hypnotist's suggestions, a deep state of somnambulism is used, passing through the first and second states of trance to get to the third, artificial somnambulism. This state is usually aimed for towards the end of the show, in order to demonstrate some of the more complicated hypnotic phenomena, such as illusions and negative and positive hallucinations. The subjects are going deeper and deeper into trance as the show goes on and in artificial somnambulism a person appears to be awake, but is actually operating under the influence of their unconscious, as opposed to their conscious mind.

The most important aspect of the third state of trance for the stage hypnotist is that it renders the volunteer into a very deep state of suggestibility. Although all people are suggestible in the other states of trance and full consciousness itself, the third state of artificial somnambulism can have a profound impact on the effectiveness of the hypnotist's suggestions.

With practice and experience the stage hypnotist learns to guide their carefully selected volunteers though the three different states of trance. They may use quickly fired suggestions to confuse the volunteer, so that they will be desperate to accept any next suggestion that comes their way.

Having said all this, there are occasions when a stage hypnotist may work with a subject in instant somnambulism before the second state has occurred, if it is a subject who naturally develops that state.

Imagination is one of the key elements that the hypnotist utilises in the subjects; the greater and more liberal the imagination the subject has, the easier they are for a hypnotist to work with. Every action is preceded by imagination; with each thing we do, we have gone through that procedure in our heads and permeated the possibilities before we have implemented the action. Some inductions may involve the volunteer imagining that they are far away on a tropical island underneath a palm tree. This occupies their conscious mind while the hypnotist gives instructions to the unconscious mind, in order to produce a trance-like state.

Bad inductions

In general when a hypnotist of any kind induces trance in a person it is considered that the induction serves to benefit the subject's state of mind. Whether the use is therapeutic, pastoral or educational does not matter, because the induction is normally a genteel process. Of course there are times when a hypnotist may use fast inductions, both to serve the needs of their clients and to save clinical, educational, or experimental time. However, to say that all inductions are totally innocuous would be incorrect.

Normally the hypnotist would choose the induction to best suit the needs of individual or group. Some inductions are not suitable for certain kinds of people. For instance a hypnotist should not use an induction that involved sleight of hand with a paranoid person, as this could make them become even more paranoid, since some of their suspicions about other's actions may have been confirmed by the trickery of the induction.

One stage induction I came across was a method of secretly administering chloroform to the subject without their prior knowledge or permission. This was done by the hypnotist hiding a spray in his sleeves and then masking the smell by using incense.

Inductions focusing on one particular sensory system could cause disturbance in a person who has a phobia rooted in that system. The clinician would have time to screen for this, but the stage hypnotist does not.

One induction involves the subject biting on a cork, and I suppose if they choked to death, it would be the manufacturer's fault for supplying a defective cork.

McGill described a very dubious induction where the hypnotist uses a secret, extremely poisonous chemical, which is rubbed onto the subject's skin to help the subject believe they are under suggestion for heat. The chemical burns the skin, the subject believes hypnosis is responsible for the heat, but because they are not told about the substance, they are given no warning not to ingest it at any time.

More advice McGill gives is in hypnotising children at parties. Fortunately some countries or states say that people cannot volunteer before the age of 18, but we know all teenagers reconstruct their age when it suits them. It has been known, however, that children have been commandeered by stage hypnotists to be subjects without their parents' permission.

Since this is not a catalogue of hypnotic inductions, but an exploration of the use of trance and hypnosis in the world of entertainment it would not be appropriate to list all the inductions used by stage hypnotists. Trance can be induced in so many different ways that it would take many more pages to complete that task.

A hypnotist can devise an induction to to suit everyone, and that is one of the superior skills that the discipline of hypnotherapy has over other therapies. The trained hypnotherapist is able to gain greater rapport with a greater number of people in a greater number of ways.

However, it also means that the stage hypnotist has countless methods to induce trance, both with the subject's and audience's conscious awareness, and without it too.

It is not important to the stage hypnotist which method of induction they use. They are show people, so what they are looking for in an induction is its entertainment value to the audience, how dramatic it looks, and how powerful it makes the stage hypnotist appear.

The trance state

It has been suggested by some clinicians and stage hypnotists alike, that the trance state is in no way harmful, but if it were truly benign then it would not prove beneficial either. It has been proved through EEG monitoring that during the state of trance the brain generally moves into alpha wave activity. This is quite different from the waking beta wave brain activity, theta activity of light sleep or delta activity of deep sleep. It is believed that during trance a large proportion of brain activity is focused in the limbic part of the brain, which contains the healing systems and the abilities to regulate the homeostasis of the body.

My observation is that the trance state is, in fact, a naturally occurring state of benefit to the body and mind, where the neocortex activity is partly closed down in order to allow healing, respite, learning and re-evaluation. Depending on the suggestions made to an individual during trance, the effects can be either beneficial or harmful. Deep states of hypnotically induced trance are generally used in varying ways for benefit to the person as a whole.

So why the stick about stage hypnosis?

In all states of trance, but particularly in the third level of artificial somnambulism, a volunteer becomes more suggestible and it is reasonably likely that a suggestion which is made to them will be turned into an action.

The suggestions that are made to stage volunteers are designed to entertain the audiences and boost the ego of the stage hypnotist, but may often be harmful to the volunteers. Since these suggestions bypass the natural critical processes that are part of the conscious mind, the filter mechanism that rejects harmful suggestions can be inoperative, because the subject is in a state of deep unconsciousness.

Suggestion Effectiveness

*"If you think you can...if you think you can't...
you're right either way".*

(Chicken Soup for the Soul volume II)

Until the development of the psychological theory of hypnosis in the latter part of the 19th century, suggestion was often discredited as being responsible for the effects produced in hypnosis. The emanations of the early magnetisers' invisible fluid were supposed to be the magic ingredient that caused any change. However, behavioural science has come a long way since then and its observations of cause and effect are well documented.

Each and every psychological, physical, medical, spiritual and philosophical discipline has a clear and defined stratagem of cause and effect.

X will or may invariably cause Y to happen.

In implementing X (a communication: suggestion through visual, auditory, kinaesthetic, olfactory or gustatory means), a hypnotist will always have in mind what they wish to have their subject do (Y). Since every individual is a different person, subjects will naturally all react in their own separate and idiosyncratic ways to any standard suggestion.

No hypnotist can forecast the *exact* reaction they will elicit from a subject. In stage hypnosis this is one of the major sources of amusement. The unpredictablity in entertainment is, after all, exciting, stimulating, fascinating and funny. People love to see their friends doing something completely out of character.

Hypnosis works on the balance of probabilities and every well-trained hypnotist understands this, making adjustments in the way they treat people in order to accommodate the odds. A hypnotherapist looks very carefully for the signs of evolvement to see if the subject is arrested at any particular stage of the development that takes place during trance. Should the subject be stuck then the hypnotherapist will take another course of action and implement further suggestions to move the client along to resolution.

The stage hypnotist will have no such goals in mind because their job is to entertain the paying public by getting a laugh and the long-term mental state of the subject is not their ultimate aim.

So let us identify the suggestion as S

The effect as EF

The short-term laughter as L

The entertainment factor as E

The mental health factor of the subject as M.

Therefore the goal of the stage hypnotist is always
$S \times EF = E$.

If possible they want $S \times EF = E + L$.

What they never want is $S \times EF = 0$ because that would mean no bookings or wages.

The hypnotherapist wants $S \times EF = M$.

The hypnotherapist can also aim for $S \times EF = M + E + L$ to make therapy fun.

The therapist can never lose sight of the M factor as a goal in order to be successful.

Stage hypnotists will forsake the M factor to get E, L or both.

All this may seem confusing to the lay person, but it is the way that some hypnotists explain how hypnosis works, especially when they are purposefully trying to confuse people in order to elevate their own intellectual status. By the way, you are now a hypnoboffin.

The bottom line is, at the expense of the long-term mental health of the subjects, the stage hypnotist will go for the cheap laughs and ignore the possible repercussions. In fact, since stage hypnotists are so good at convincing their subjects and audiences that things are not there (negative hallucinations), they may ignore the risks, making them invisible to their subjects, themselves and anyone who challenges their motives.

What risks?...I see no risks...can you see any risks?

Meet my friend, the expert...he sees no risks (probably because his views are contrary to the other 99% of the hypnotherapy community)...so you will see no risks.
Will you?

Hypnotic suggestions and moral codes
It has been proposed by some hypnotists that if a suggestion is made to a subject, which is contrary to that person's moral code or belief system, it will not be effective. They believe the unconscious mind will reject, countermand or cancel such a suggestion.

Erickson carried out experiments to determine to what extent a subject may be persuaded to cross their moral code. His results were that he believed the subject's unconscious protective mechanisms cut in to countermand all harmful suggestions. However, such experiments are usually carried out under laboratory conditions and produce artificial results. Furthermore the extent to which an experimenter may use contraindicated suggestions to a subject is limited by the moral and ethical guidelines that such experimenters must operate under. To exceed those guidelines would find the experimenter in a position of being an abuser and no longer an experimenter.

Not all hypnotic experimenters have held the same view. In 1887 Liébeault induced a young man to steal under the influence of a post-hypnotic suggestion (Gauld 1992). Two months later the young man was caught stealing an overcoat. He also had in his possession a notebook detailing his stealing events. Liébeault later discovered that the young man had been instructed to steal by another doctor at the original experiment.

Liebeault believed that his own original suggestion had instilled a stealing impulse. He conjectured that the original suggestion might have failed had the young man been of good moral character, but that argument must be ignored because the judgement of a moral character is purely a subjective estimation. Each of us have our own concept of morality that only loosely corresponds to the socially orientated collective moral code. The true facts of the experiment are that the young man had been induced to steal.

Hypnotists who have worked for the CIA and other secretive powerful organisations have reported that they have used hypnotised subjects to carry out acts of assassination and implemented amnesia in the subjects, to take place after the event.

So were those subjects then going against their own deep moral code?

Had they been influenced beyond what would normally have been acceptable to them?

It seems that in such cases the unconscious mind had not kick-started the defence system that would normally protect the subject from a suggestion that might be against their greater good.

Or was their concept of their greater good associated with the detriment of their victim?

There are also recorded cases of victims of hypnosis, where the hypnotist has taken sexual advantage of the subject while they were under hypnosis. The majority of these are where the hypnotist is a male seducer of a female subject and commits the act of rape, often creating amnesia in the subject so they remember nothing consciously.

In such cases it is often some time before the facts of the events become known to the victim — days weeks, or even years. Again the subject's unconscious mind was not operating its normal protective defence mechanisms and the harm that was perpetrated against the victim might not have been allowed had they been in the conscious waking state.

I believe a hypnotist may use a suggestion that could harm a subject and that subject would accept it. A hypnotist may frame a suggestion in such a way that they associate the desired action to an already existing acceptable idea. This is one of the main principles of hypnosis, that of empathy, and the very first premise that the hypnotist must take on board in order to get in rapport with their subjects.

Empathy must always be maintained during the hypnotic process and the hypnotist who is a skilled linguist and behaviourist can frame suggestions in a way that is acceptable to the subject.

To see this as purely an ability held by a hypnotist to implant ideas into the subject's mind would be incorrect. The nature of suggestion is such that it is a process that takes place in all human interaction on many levels. We frame our communications to get across our meaning and to cause an outcome to happen in our natural waking state. We have presupposed before we implement a communication that we wish something to happen and then we frame our communication in order to make that happen.

The hypnotist, because of their deep understanding of the way to frame communications so the subject will find them acceptable, is able to lead a person into believing things that are not normally acceptable to their conscious mind. The stage hypnotist has learnt how to do this, but does not understand the long-term implications of their suggestions. For them this is a tool that they use in order to get their subjects to be entertaining.

> *You are a chicken that thinks it is a dog*
> *and every woman you see will appear to be a cat*
> *and you will try to chase her up a tree*

For the hypnotherapist it is a tool with which they help their subjects to arrive at desired point of development. Not, of course, helping a person to think that they are a chicken that thinks it is a dog, but to perhaps help someone believe they have more confidence than they used to have. Evolving a subject's development requires an understanding of the human mind, and not just knowing how to get a laugh.

Studies have indicated that it is possible to change attitudes and beliefs to an alarming degree (Asch 1952, 1956; Milgram 1974; Orne & Evans, 1965). Hypnosis is a tool that can be used to activate such changes and some studies say that it is no more effective than conscious coercion

(Coe, Kobayashi, & Howard 1973; Orne & Evans, 1965). However, we must consider that if the communication is within the context of hypnosis, then not only do the beliefs and attitudes change, but the belief that they were altered by hypnosis will also exist.

Negative and positive hallucinations

A negative hallucination is not seeing something which is there. Usually at the end of the show the hypnotist will attempt a negative hallucination, with a very receptive subject, using a set-up like the flying child. The subject, while in the second state of trance, is told that when they wake up they will not see the stage hypnotist at all. A child is called for from the audience and duly held in the air above the hypnotist's head as he or she walks across the stage. The subject is told to wake up and when they do, all that they can see is the child flying across the stage. Their startled, puzzled and shocked reactions amuse the audience greatly.

When you awaken you will see a flying nymph

A positive hallucination is seeing something which is not there. This is demonstrated by telling the subject that they will see something that is not there when they wake up. Of course they are not waking up into the normal conscious state but into the artificial somnambulistic state of deep trance. If the hypnotist uses a lion and the subject stands on their chair in fear of being eaten this causes an uproar and the audience goes into raptures of laughter.

When you awaken you will be at the zoo in the lions' cage

Variations on the demonstrations of negative and positive hallucinations are always included in the show, as they are very popular, since the audience are fascinated and cannot understand how this is done.

When you wake up you will have two penises

When you awaken the audience will have no clothes on

Another hypnotic phenomenon that is used is the alteration of sensory perception, where an individual generates sensation or converts one into another. These conversion mechanisms are taking place at a deep unconscious level, out of conscious of awareness.

When you wake up I am going to give you an onion...but you will believe it is a lovely red apple...and you are hungry for a nice red apple

When I wake you up you will think your breasts are on fire...you will put as many icecubes as you can in your bra to cool you down

A Pavlovian stimulus and reponse behaviour pattern can be demonstrated too, again making the stage hypnotist appear to have great powers.

When I say the word "banana" you will look at the nearest man to you...and ask him to take you...then you will have the biggest orgasm you have ever had

Fractionation
As mentioned earlier stage hypnotists often use the fractionation technique, where the subject is continually woken up and put back into trance. Each time the subject is woken up they are given a task to do to amuse the audience and then told that it will also make them go deeper and deeper into trance.

When I snap my fingers
you are going to pretend you are a washing machine...
you are on the fast spin cycle...
and with each rotation you will go deeper and deeper into trance

As the subject throws themselves around the audience is highly amused, the trance is deepened, the confusion and fractionation continues and the subject believes more and more that they are under the stage hypnotist's power. With the washing machine suggestion there have been reports of long-term stomach upsets in some subjects.

> *When you are awakened your hands will revolve in circles around each other...*
> *they will get faster and faster and faster...*
> *and you will go deeper with each turn*

Not everyone who is susceptible to hypnosis is comfortable with the continual confusion of going to sleep and then being woken up. For some people this is most disturbing and they develop feelings of being rendered powerless, finding the experience oppressive and even ego damaging. They are usually unable consciously to protest and even if they do manage this, the stage hypnotist is unlikely to take any notice.

The rapid succession of tasks that the subjects are required to perform in such a short space of time is disorientating for some. They become very upset and stressed, particularly as they retain little conscious memory of what has happened to them.

Another complication that occurs with stage hypnotists is that they have no training in the use of language and symbolism and use the kind of inductions and suggestions that could be harmful.

> *You are sinking down, down...deep...into the black abyss...*
> *Deeper and deeper into the black abyss...*

Any well-trained therapist would know not to use phrases like this because it is the kind of language that depressed people bring to therapy. A large percentage of the severely depressed people I have met talk about a feeling of blackness and sinking into an abyss. To suggest this to a person who is in trance is asking for trouble, but the stage hypnotis does not have the knowledge to avoid such *faux pas*.

Internet suggestions

On the 28th November 1996 I lifted the following suggestions off the internet. They were posted in order to give ideas to stage hypnotists about what kind of suggestions they could use in their shows.

You are a sex goddess; everyone wants you

Advise all the subjects that on the count of three, they will become the opposite sex

You are a smoker...when you have a smoke...it will taste like burning rubber

You are the first man that may have breast cancer. Two women on the stage will now check you for lumps

*You have forgotten what sex you are...
You know that you are either male or female...
but you cannot recall which one you are*

*You have just found out that you are gay...
You will look out in the audience and find someone that looks good to you*

Hypnotic suggestions affect each of us in an individual way, and the effectiveness is dependent upon how we filter the acceptability of that suggestion through our own subjective psychological constructs. The science of behavioural alteration, through hypnotic suggestion, is a process of working with the subjects through a continual complex of mental actions and reactions.

There is no standard formula that is categorically effective with everyone, every time. What will be effective with one subject will invariably be ineffective with another, therefore the hypnotist will have to try something different. The stage hypnotist does not have time to go through this process with each individual subject and relies upon one suggestion being suitable for all — but this can never be.

Illusions

It is important here to clearly differentiate between illusions and hallucinations. An illusion is an altered perception of existing circumstances, objects or persons. A hallucination is the sensory perception of something that is not actually there or the deletion of something that is there. Since illusions are an easier hypnotic phenomenon for a subject to experience they will come earlier in a show than hallucinations.

However, for the subjects who can become instantly somnambulistic it is easy to give them suggestions to produce hallucinations without taking them through the official trance induction. To the audience this seems amazing, but we must remember that they may be one of the most suggestible subjects from the committee. Some stage hypnotists use this kind of hallucination with the instant somnambulists to convince the committee that trance exists.

Dysmorphobia

One of the most controversial sets of suggestions that stage hypnotists use is the removal of body parts. Although this suggestion is prohibited in some places stage hypnotists often find a way to get around it.

When you wake up you will have no penis

Just as you step off the stage...

and go back to the audience...
you will find you are looking under the tables for your
breasts

These suggestions can have long-lasting, devastating effects on some of the subjects and can cause a condition called dysmorphobia. This is when a person is unhappy with their own body image and is common to anorexia, bulimia, polysurgery, Gender Dysphoria and self-harming. While this condition can be brought on by a physiological condition in the body, it can also be induced through psychological distortion.

False Memory Syndrome
The recording of false, harmful information in the memory banks of the mind occurs when another person makes suggestions that may cause false memories or perceptions about the past, present or even future (Spanos 1996). It has been a particularly high-profile syndrome, concerning adults who, while in therapy, have suddenly remembered they suffered child abuse. However, this was not the case, but the therapist's careless use of suggestion had led the individual to believe that the abuse happened. It is something that many therapists all over the world are now being sued for doing.

I am not saying that stage hypnotists necessarily induce memories of childhood abuse, although they can; what I am saying is that they can induce any false memories through careless use of suggestion. Therapists use False Memory Syndrome postively as a technique to implant good memories in the past of a disturbed client (Erickson 1989) and this is accepted as valid. However, if someone is using hypnosis and suggestion they must be very careful about what they are suggesting; it should not be a flippant procedure.

Regression
In regression a subject is taken back to an earlier age. In some places this is banned in stage hypnosis, but again

stage hypnotists have found ways of getting around the ban simply by suggesting that the subject is another four-year-old. Since there is no screening procedure in stage hypnosis, repressed memories, which may be traumatic for the subject to deal with consciously, can surface during a performance.

You are four years old again in the classroom and some-one has upset you...you start balling your eyes out

An audience finds it hilarious to see a 20-stone, 50-year-old man crying his eyes out as if he were a four-year-old child. It represents the very essence of entertainment, the epoch of commedia dell' arte. However, the man may have had a traumatic time when he was four years old. His unconscious may have taken many years and great care to file those memories away safely, so as not to disturb his present life. Since the stage hypnotist knows nothing about that person, they are tampering with dynamite.

Amnesia
Amnesia for a person's own identity (depersonalisation) can be brought about through hypnotic suggestion. In therapy this can be useful at times to help a client forget traumatic parts of their own history or disturbing sub-personalities. But to use this to entertain an audience can leave a person with a deficit in their identity.

When you wake up you will completely forget your own name...address...and identity

Catalepsy
Through suggestion the hypnotist can produce catalepsy in the subjects. This is when the muscles seem to have part or whole of the subject frozen and motionless. In partial catalepsy limbs may be placed in a particular position and will remain there undisturbed by the normal fatigue experienced in the waking state. Comedy can be produced

by visually disempowering the subjects and placing them in funny positions.

In total catalepsy the hypnotist suggests that all the muscles in the body become completely stiff and rigid. These suggestions are often accompanied by various mesmeric passes of hands over the body that are not only convincing to the subject but also very visual for entertainment purposes. For this the hypnotist will choose the most receptive of their subjects, who will respond to virtually all the commands given. The subject, having become completely stiff like a board, can then be suspended between two surfaces, the head touching one end, the feet the other. This demonstration of the effect that the mind can have over the body is known as the human plank trick.

Abreactions

An abreaction is what takes place when things go wrong. It can be a psychological or physical reaction that ranges from crying all the way to a heart attack. Abreactions are usually the result of over provocative or dangerous suggestions that can evoke distress in the subject. Repressed memories or fears may suddenly surface into consciousness causing great distress and wild reactions. There is also the danger that wrongful suggestion may cause abreactions to take place on a post-hypnotic basis.

If it occurs in the clinical situation it can be dealt with effectively by a properly trained therapist, returning the subject to full functional ability. A therapist takes all reasonable precautions to deal with the unexpected abreaction that can occur during an induction and maintenance of hypnosis, but a stage hypnotist not only takes few precautions, they also may have very little knowledge about what is actually happening. They have neither the time nor the attention to pay to one particular individual. This means that an abreaction can go un-noticed, sometimes getting out of hand and causing long-term mental problems in the subject.

There are many scenarios and antics that the stage hypnotist gets up to that I have not covered, because they are too diverse and would take up a whole book in themselves. What I have tried to do is give the reader a general idea of the kind of suggestions that are being used by stage hypnotists, the context in which they are used, and some of the effects and consequences that these suggestions invoke.

Post-hypnotic suggestion

Looking at the use of post-hypnotic suggestion in stage hypnosis requires us to define what exactly is meant by this phrase. Standard post-hypnotic suggestion is where a suggestion is made to the subject, while they are in one of the states of trance, to perform the action suggested when they wake up. The kind of post-hypnotic suggestion that is used in stage hypnosis is different to that used in the clinical setting in so far as the action is not performed in the waking state but in the artificial somnambulistic state of deep trance.

Each time you reach your seat...you will remember you have forgotten your scarf...you will return to the stage and I will put another scarf around your neck

If the person is still in trance when they have performed the action derived from the suggestion, I shall call it **intrahypnotic suggestion**. The stage hypnotist claims to cancel all suggestions before the person is brought out of trance and back to the normal conscious waking state.

However, a bone of contention arises here depending on a person's view of the ability of a hypnotist to control their subject's actions. The stage hypnotist contests that they can and do cancel all suggestions that may cause difficulty to the subjects, before the end of each show. I find this an incredibly arrogant and unscientific assumption, based on the hypnotist's efficacy of their own self-importance.

With hypnosis the hypnotist makes suggestions that work on the balance of probability. As mentioned earlier not every suggestion made to a subject will cause an action to take place. Quite often the hypnotist will settle

for a different action other that the one originally suggested (the unpredictability principle). Naturally a hypnotist is
trying the get the majority of their suggestions that they
give to a subject turned into actions, but there are no
guarantees.

Therefore, logically we can now consider that if a hypnotist cannot guarantee a suggestion turning into an
action, neither can they be certain that the cancellation of
a suggestion will be completely effective either. Of course
it appears to the audience or the onlooker that the stage
hypnotist can get 100% response because they are creating that illusion through entertainment.

There is the further consideration that the stage hypnotist's limited knowledge of the psychological disciplines
leaves them without the ability to anticipate the possible
repercussions for uncancelled suggestions. What may
have been originally conceived as intrahypnotic suggestions by the stage hypnotist could, in reality, turn into
post-hypnotic suggestions, and as my research shows,
sometimes does.

Through experience and knowledge the clinical hypnotist estimates that the majority of their suggestions can
evoke a desired reaction. During the course of therapy the
therapist uses a series of suggestions that are directed
towards helping a client resolve their problems. At times
that may include the induction of one of the hypnotic phenomena, including catalepsy, analgesia, anaesthesia,
amnesia, illusions, positive or negative hallucinations, and
alterations of sensory perceptions. Never do they induce
those phenomena in order to purely entertain or amuse
others.

In clinical demonstration hypnosis professional hypnotists take great care not to ridicule, humiliate or cause
embarrassment to the subjects, having their mental
health as the prime consideration. The process may
include sharing humour with the subject, but never sub-
jecting them to ridicule.

Suggestion can be so powerful that even McGill wrote
about a young American student who, he believed, was

undoubtedly killed by its power. At an American university, during a fraternity initiation ceremony, a young man was blindfolded and was told his head was going to be chopped off.

Then the young man's neck was placed on a block, and in full expectation of the above suggestion, he found something bearing down on the back of his neck. It was, in fact, only a wet towel, but he died of a heart attack nevertheless. He was obviously in some state of trance, very open to suggestion, and the mere contact evoked a physiological reaction as a result of the psychological suggestion.

Another example of the power of post-hypnotic suggestion is discussed in Chapter 7: Reviewing the Sharron Tabarn Case.

The more the world population centres around urban sprawls, the greater the pressure grows on individuals and families to escape the stress of the modern city dwelling. Humour, out of all the emotions, is the one that breaks the ice most effectively when the friction of constant exposure to other humans has set in. The highest priority of the stage hypnotist is to get a laugh; amazement may be the second, but without the first they will not get a second booking. To that ends the stage hypnotist will be prepared to go to any lengths in order to earn their living.

After such a statement, I can already hear the scribbling of pens on paper of the stage hypnotists composing their protestations and mailing them to me. To them I ask: Can count the ways you have had to get a laugh during a bad matinée, when it is snowing and only the front three rows are full? Among the suggestions you have used, do you really, hand on heart, know the long-term effects?

There is, after all, absolutely no follow-up. Certainly it is unlikely they will ever see their subjects again.

I close this chapter with the very words of McGill himself:

"The extraordinary phenomenon of hypnotism is like a game you play.
Sometimes you win and sometimes you lose"

(The New Encyclopaedia of Stage Hypnotism p 258)

4

The History of Stage Hypnosis

As we saw earlier, hypnosis is what we culturally call the trance-like relationship between two or more people, and even in self-hypnosis our state changes as we alter the way the different parts of ourselves interrelate. Each of us are not only bound by our personal interpretation of what hypnosis is, but also our cultural understanding. Moving from one culture or time to another changes the classification of what may or may not constitute hypnosis.

Chinese medicine recognises over 5000 years of hypnotic relationships between healers and patients. The Egyptians experienced Temple Sleep, which was induced and identified by priests as a special healing and enlightening state. In ancient Greece, Asclepian dream healing could also contextually be identified as hypnosis. Moses, Jesus, Mohammed, Ghengis Khan, Richard the Lionheart, Napoleon, Hitler, Churchill, and Billy Graham, all practised hypnosis from a socio-psychological perspective and expansionist point of view. Tribal medicine men, witch-doctors, Hindu fakirs, Indian yogi and Persian magi have all practised their own forms of hypnosis, either consciously or unconsciously, not necessarily having identified it as hypnosis.

Generally this ability to entrance and utilise that special focused relationship has remained in the hands of spiritual leaders, priests, healers and philosophers. Hypnosis has been a tool that many civilisations have used either to control the many or guide, cure and develop the individual. I can find no reference to anything vaguely similar to stage hypnosis for entertainment before the last 200 years. However, magicians have used hypnotic components in the way they work, throughout the ages, to perpetuate their myths of mystical powers.

Animal magnetism (mesmerism)

The first high-profile use of hypnosis in our modern records is with the physician Anton Mesmer (1734-1815). His theory of animal magnetism included the passing of hands over parts of the subject's body, which was supposed to effect a cure. His patients believed that he was transferring a magnetic force or invisible fluid into them that would travel around their bodies to dispel illness. This force could be stored in many objects and receptacles to be used when needed, and could be transferred either through the hands or sometimes a metal wand. Far from being purely the result of the placebo effect, Mesmer believed that such a force actually existed. He wrote a very important scientific paper considering magnet influences on the movements of the sun, moon and planets and on human health.

With great ceremony the subjects receiving the treatment sat in a large wooden tub called a baquet, into which were threaded iron rods that were supposedly magnetised. This all took place in an atmospherically light room, often with mood music playing, and generally the setting was compliant with Mesmer's understanding of how best to help the patient believe in the cure.

Mesmer learnt his ability to perform the basics of his form of mesmerism from a Catholic priest who practised exorcism, and he trained in the priesthood himself before taking up medicine. Not only did he become aware of the mechanics of persuasion that the priest was using, but he also took on the concept of magnetic transference that was popular at the time.

Many of the subjects of animal magnetism believed they saw the fluid or force flowing into them and around them, even without suggestion from the operator. The subjects' own expectations induced hallucinations of the magnetic force and it was often quoted as being blue. This force could supposedly be transferred from one object to another. Water that was believed to be magnetised was imbued with the power of sending a person into trance when drinking it, and therefore, by implication did just that.

The success of Mesmer's clinic in Paris caused the proliferation of many imitators of his spectacular cures. Only some understood the full force and effectiveness of the hypnotist's personality, coupled with the careful use of suggestion. Due to the many recorded cures it was difficult for his enemies and doubters to publicly dismiss Mesmer out of hand.

The Society of Harmony that he formed was sworn not to reveal the way in which cures were achieved. Some of his followers, after completing his training course, were still none the wiser as to how his theory of animal magnetism worked.

One of his followers, the Marquis De Puységur (1751-1825), was one of the earliest recorded hypnotists to purposefully use the artificial somnambulistic state. There are cases where Puységur took the subject into this state, and allowed their unconscious to diagnose and prescribe their own ailments and cures. This later became part of the way hypnotherapists use the unconscious to understand what is going on out of conscious awareness.

While Mesmer's fame made him a very comfortable and successful living, many of his disciples did not charge for their services. Animal magnetism was considered a way of helping the diseased and tormented, and although it was demonstrated, it was not classed as entertainment. As the practice of using the artificial somnambulistic state to diagnose and prescribe spread, the favourite subjects of the magnetisers, who went easily into deep trances, were used to diagnosis the illness and treatment of others too.

Many of the magnetisers now began to realise that it was the hypnotic placebo effect that was responsible for alleviating psychosomatic illness, and that it could be reproduced without any connection to the magnetism. The artificial somnambulistic trance began to be used by clairvoyants, fortune tellers, masons and even a diversity of religious spiritualists.

It was the catastrophic effects of the French Revolution

that diluted mesmerism's popular interest in France. Many of the proponents and personalities who performed animal magnetism were either wiped out or too preoccupied, after the revolution to continue practising or researching it.

Mesmerism spread to the German-speaking world and was accepted well, in some parts, by the medical profession. Various experiments were published surmising that its healing power was due to the transference of electrical forces being moved around the body. Others were less happy with this theory and went to train with Puységur at the Strasbourg Society of Harmony, who was more inclined to the psychological theory of healing.

The spread of mesmerism throughout the German-speaking world was due initially to the masons, but religious orders and mystics soon claimed their portion of the action. Mesmer, who had retired to Switzerland after the French Revolution, was invited to Berlin in 1811 to demonstrate animal magnetism in the hospital there, but he declined the offer on grounds of health and old age. By this time, the mysticism surrounding the use of mesmerism had so worried the Berlin Head of the Department of Police, that he issued an order forbidding anyone to practice animal magnetism unless they were medically qualified.

K C Wolfart (1778-1832) was made the first professor of animal magnetism and although there were doubters, many German doctors were taking the treatment seriously. In Austria, however, it was banned, but continued to go on away from the eye of officialdom.

Russia, at the beginning of the 19th century, saw the spread of animal magnetism as it became very popular, until in 1816 it had been restricted to the medical profession. There was some Scandinavian interest but this was mainly in Sweden and was very short-lived. In Holland and Belgium there was also some interest, but again this was thin on the ground.

After the revolution in France animal magnetism was not resurrected again until 1813-1814 onwards when it was mainly in the hands of enthusiastic amateurs, who also published papers about their work. However, in the 1820s it became of great interest to the medical establishment; and lectures were held and it was used in hospitals.

The topical debate among the medical fraternity still questioned whether there really was some strange magnetic force involved, being passed from the magnetiser to the subject. There were practitioners who were not comfortable with the label of magnetiser, separating the practice from any notion of the unquantifiable, invisible magnetic fluid that supposedly flowed as part of the healing process.

The professional artificial somnambulists, who put themselves into trances to diagnose other people's illnesses and prescribe a cure, also flourished, cloaked in clouds of mysticism, as did clairvoyants and fortune tellers. Eventually a damning report on animal magnetism in 1840 caused the medical profession in Paris to abandon the practice and it was left in the hands of the professional somnambulists.

In German-speaking countries as well, animal magnetism drifted towards the esoteric with the advent of romanticism. Somnambulists were given to talking to the spirits, linking them directly to God, and many paranormal phenomena were recorded in connection with mediumship. Right up until the 1850s masonry and professional somnambuls took animal magnetism away from the realms of science, veiling it instead in the shrouds of the occult or extraterrestrial. At times there could be very be overtly controlling relationships between male controllers and their female, professional somnambulists.

It was suggested in some quarters that the ability for somnambulists to go into trance was an indicator of a weak or partially diseased nervous system. Critics of stories about divine communicating, such as Fischer and Wirth, contested the reality of such experiences and explained them as being part of the imaginative psychological process.

Out of the romantic period came the seeding concepts of the conscious and unconscious mind, which, in the second half of the 19th century, firmed up as part of the postulates of hypnotism. Much debate continued with the split between the theorists and the mystics, the latter developing into the birth of the modern spiritualist movement around 1850.

Lafontaine (1803-1892) travelled widely in France and abroad demonstrating magnetism, after having trained in Brussels. Unlike the other travelling demonstrators giving public performances, he came from a theatrical background, and entertainingly performed to audiences of hundreds of people. Part of his act involved soliciting a member of the audience, mesmerising them and then demonstrating various hypnotic phenomena. These could include desensitisation to pain, being prodded with needles, or rendering the subjects impartial to the sound of gun shots or foul smells. He was so confident in his performances that he was able to play to sceptical, rowdy crowds, even in places where animal magnetism was banned.

The French medical profession was so disturbed by the practice of animal magnetism by non medical people that in 1845 the Congress Medical De Paris voted that only doctors should be allowed to practise it. Many lay magnetisers were thereafter prosecuted for illegally performing medicine. A great deal of interest from all over the world was still demonstrated by orders for the magnetism periodicals, which only seemed to survive through foreign subscriptions.

Towards the end of the first half of the 19th century animal magnetism spread as far as Italy, Spain, Corfu, throughout the rest of Europe and Scandinavia, and even Brazil. This spread was patchy and, at times, encountered resistance from the Catholic Church, which believed that the clairvoyant elements of trance work needed to be prevented. In Rome and Naples animal magnetism was banned and in Lombardy only medical professionals were allowed to practise it.

The travellers who demonstrated magnetism did so in a mainly medical manner, but they often went on to elicit mystical qualities from their subjects. In considering this in a historical context we must remember that their comprehension of medicine, science, psychology and philosophy was relative to their time and culture, and quite different from our late 20th-century perspectives.

Those who were now not allowed to practise as professional somnambulists were going under the identity of travelling clairvoyants. They enjoyed the reputation of finding lost property, locating dead bodies, detecting criminals and solving crimes. Still today those who set themselves up as clairvoyants, travelling fortune tellers and mystics make claims and predictions for the public. They often do this by going into trance and then connecting with a class of guides, which they claim are unavailable to the average person.

Even now the police in different parts of the world including Bali, England, America, India, France, Russia and Hong Kong still consult these mystics, and secretly enlist their help in investigations.

Mesmerism arrived in the United States later, around the 1830s onwards, as America began to get carried away with the adventurous optimism of the land of opportunity and exploration. Once again various demonstrators toured, giving instruction on its medical applications. The arrival of the magnetisers from France, like Charles Poyen St. Sauveur brought with them the knowledge that would spread. Although interest was slow at first, around 1837 his lectures became very well attended and the publicity surrounding him led to great enthusiasm for mesmerism.

A class of professional prophets, who spoke about the benefits and advantages of mesmerism arose and there were many lectures and demonstrations given as the country was taken with magnetism fever. Many professional magnetisers soon appeared and it was estimated that in Boston alone there were more than 200. Some of the professional magnetisers had received no longer than 10 hours of training.

Two demonstrators in particular, Dods and Grimes, were very apt at inducing positive or negative hallucinations with hypersuggestible subjects, without the need for formal inductions. These particular phenomena were the central core of the performances of the next generation of demonstrators, who formed the first official stage hypnosis acts.

The doctrine of the electrobiologists, who were a theoretical subversion of animal magnetisers, was the first clearly defined example of the practical applications of mind over matter. Their acts also consisted of a cross between demonstrations of hypnosis and the demonstration of the new phenomenon of electricity.

Academia, the medical fraternity and the scientific world stole away secretly to watch these shows, and were able to take from them the principles which were to make up the psychological theories of hypnosis. Instead of the magnetiser passing the magnetic force into the subject's body, the subject was simply asked to concentrate on a coin for five to ten minutes while they were being talked to.

In Britain animal magnetism appeared shortly after Mesmer's appearance in Paris, but no publication on the subject can be found before 1784. Schools were set up to teach it, but the fees were so high that it was mainly kept to the wealthier classes. French animal magnetism had a great influence and and interest became high again after the French Revolution ended. It was the late 1820s before any real interest in the medical usage of magnetism surfaced under the operator Richard Chenevix (1774-1830). His demonstrations of cures witnessed by eminent medical men of the time were reported in *The London Physical and Medical Journal*.

A French demonstrator, Baron Dupont, came to England in 1837 and fired the interest of John Elliotson, the professor of the practice of medicine at London University and senior physician at University College Hospital. Since Elliotson was such an eminent, respected medical man, his enthusiasm about the practice of animal magnetism spread outside the profession. He was so taken with mesmerism that when the hospital committees banned its use on their wards he resigned both from the college and hospital, never to return.

The Rev Chauncy Hare Townshend, a much travelled

man, published his book *Facts in Mesmerism,* which was the first of many ecclesiastical publications to influence public opinion at this time.

The arrival of Charles La Fontaine, the French magnetic demonstrator, in 1841 caused great publicity with his well-attended demonstrations all over the country. He particularly demonstrated the hypnotic phenomenon of sensory alteration, where the hypnotised subject is unable to consciously perceive physical discomfort or pain.

Many imitators sprang up and also gave public demonstrations to hundreds and sometimes thousands of people. The popularity of magnetism now expounded with many publications being translated from the French. Practical guides in English appeared, culminating in the peak of popularity in the early 1850s.

In 1848 the second edition of Sandby's *Mesmerism and its Opponents* (Gauld 1992) was published with 81 practitioners listed, divided up into medical men, clergymen, professional men, others of independent means, mesmeric lecturers, demonstrators, and people whose status was unknown. No mention is made of anyone who uses mesmerism for entertainment purposes. The demise of mesmerism in England came about in the 1850s mainly because of the arrival of chemical anaesthetics, the retirement of Elliotson and the arrival of spiritualism from America.

The essence of suggestion in mesmerism had always been noted and capitalised on, even by Mesmer himself, and maybe this is an element of his induction process that he might fairly have been accused of not passing on to his students. Puységur had pursued the psychological angle of the mesmeric treatment that he and his students applied. However, there were many who hung onto the magnetism theory of trance induction until the bitter end.

As happened abroad the mystical elements of mesmerism split off in many directions in England, as professional somnambulists, who were forbidden from practising by the medical profession in many places, moved into clairvoyancy, mysticism and eventually spiritualism. The ceremonial magic elements of trance work continued and flourished in the masons and lodge societies. At times religion too utilised the trances states as an additional ministerial tool, sometimes citing it as diabolic, according to their needs.

The emergence of the brief period of electrobiology removed any need for the concept of the magnetic force. It recognised that the power of the operator's personality was a large constituent in the successfulness of taking the subject into trance. The demonstrations of the electrobiologists H G Darling and others, around 1850, clearly showed that it was not even necessary to put a subject into trance to induce many of the hypnotic phenomena we know today.

After seeing such demonstrations the medical fraternity were much more comfortable with a theory of mind over matter. However, mesmerism began to die out as science progressed and it looked less and less likely that the magnetic fluid existed in any form. Progress in the mechanical understanding of the body and the nervous system moved the focus of cures away from the mysterious to the development of psychosomatic knowledge.

In the second half of the 19th century magnetism fell in popularity and the psychological theory of hypnosis established itself. James Braid, the English doctor, coined the word "hypnosis", and the first International Congress of Hypnotism was held in Paris in 1889, at the same time as the few remaining magnetisers held their conference.

There is no doubt that some of the early magnetisers could be identified as stage performers in the way they conducted their public demonstrations. The Abbé José-Custodio de Faria (1756-1819), a failed priest and later a professor of philosophy at the Lycée of Marseilles, was quite a showman. Much of his demonstrations were similar to the kind of hypnotic phenomena we see in the stage shows of the late 20th century. He decried the theory of the magnetic fluid, ardently believing that the results which were produced in his subjects were due solely to his personality and use of suggestion, coupled with the subject's desire to conform.

He demonstrated positive and negative hallucinations, sensory alteration, catalepsy, anaesthesia and the illusion of turning water into intoxicating fluids (drunk by suggestion). He did very well until 1815 when certain clergymen denounced him as a sorcerer. He was also condemned by the Societé du Magnétisme as a fraud and eventually forced to close his salon in 1816.

The Rev La Roy Sunderland (1804-1905) of America developed and demonstrated his own style of hypnosis, which he called "pathetism". He would induce in his subjects many of the entertaining hypnotic phenomena to please an audience, exhibiting catalepsy, anaesthesia, singing, dancing and visions of dead friends and religious figures. He also went on to demonstrate clairvoyancy, mind reading, hallucinations, muscle rigidity and even allowed subjects to undergo minor operations during the performance.

Carl Hansen (1833-1897) was a prolific magnetic demonstrator who travelled to many countries including Sweden, Finland, Russia, France, Germany, Austria and Britain. Because of his popularity and his public profile he also attracted a considerable number of the scientific gentlemen of the day to his demonstrations.

Being a very talented hypnotist he added to the usual repertoire by placing his subjects in ridiculous cataleptic postures and making them eat potatoes believing they were pears. He also induced intoxication by imaginary consumption in his volunteers as well as performing the human plank trick. His competence made him well known for his ability to induce post-hypnotic suggestions and his performances were so repeatable that it could be said that he influenced the way many of those using hypnosis in medicine worked.

The stage hypnotists became more prevalent towards the end of the 19th century as they polished their acts. A so-called "Doctor Bodie" combined hypnosis with electrical wizardry, but he was not actually a doctor, although, as long as he was entertaining his audiences, they did not seem to care about his charlatanism. Madam Card was another popular performing hypnotist, who entertained and entranced the undergraduates of Cambridge.

In order to fascinate and enthral their audiences the performing magnetic demonstrators sought to amuse and amaze often more along theatrical lines than scientific education. They learned very early on, that providing they could avoid accusations of diabolic practices, drawing such large crowds could prove financially rewarding. Presenting what appeared to be magical was guaranteed to be popular, as long it escaped the attention of the state or the church. Stage hypnotism was much more closely aligned with conjuring, magicianship, mysticism, and at times, the occult, as even things like levitation may have been included in the act.

The illusionary nature of the stage hypnotists' developed, elevated authoritarian powers, at times, appeals to the aspirations and helplessness in all of us. In our journey through life we want to believe that there are more powers available than are presently known to our own conscious minds.

With the emergence of psychoanalysis at the end of the 19th century, the rise of clinical psychology and the increase of the waking psychotherapeutic talking therapies, hypnosis lost much of its popularity around this time. A continuing intellectual debate as to whether hypnosis was, in fact, a special state became the focus at psychological symposiums. While its popularity among the healing professions withered, hypnotists such as Vogt of Germany continued to present it as an evocative and effective clinical tool.

Although stage hypnotists often claim that during times like these it is they who keep the skills and art of hypnosis alive, this simply is not true. As we survey the history of hypnosis there are always those in the curative disciplines who are not only using hypnosis, but are developing and experimenting too.

At many times, including the beginning of the 20th century, when hypnosis falls out of favour, there are concerted efforts to categorise it as a pathology of mind, body or spirit. These kind of efforts are not driven by explicit investigations of hypnosis, but always by theorists who have their alternative methodologies to promote. Stage hypnosis, with its similarity to magic, mysticism and trickery, supplies the perfect ammunition for those with competitive agendas to disembowel hypnosis as a whole.

The Harry Price collection
Naturally to cover all the international and intercultural aspects of stage hypnosis would demand many volumes and is beyond the space and guidelines of this book. However, as I continued to look at the way stage hypnosis developed as a form of entertainment my research took me to the Harry Price collection at the University of London. The sheer size and variety of the collection tells us something in itself about the sociological aspects of the growth of hypnosis in general. The volumes included works on mesmerism, hypnosis in medicine and curing disease, hypnotherapy, treating insanity, psychotherapy, spiritualism, clairvoyancy, astrology, occultism, hysteria, magic, illusion, religion, Hinduism, electrobiology and home uses of hypnosis

The popular use of hypnosis in entertainment and its public image led to Dr Ernest Hart writing a paper entitled *"Hypnotism and Humbug* (1892), in which he asks if hypnosis is still in the same grooves of ignorance, superstition, knavery, folly and self-deception. He cited its use as not being worthy of recognition and serious scientific stature.

The paper prompted a reply by Bramwell, MB of the York Medical Society, who submitted it to the British Medical Journal the same year. He spoke of how, in Britain, hypnotism had not gained the credibility for therapeutic purposes that it had on the continent, because of the way its practitioners presented it. He disputed that its rejection was due to antagonism by the medical profession. However the president of the Royal College of Surgeons condemned hypnosis, even though he had quite frankly admitted that he was almost entirely ignorant of the subject.

Secrets of Stage Hypnotism, Stage Electricity and Bloodless Surgery (1912) by J F Burrows, a hypnotist whose stage name was Karlyn, was published by a magic company in London. The introduction talks of the author's success in the variety theatre and how it appears to be the most popular act on the billing. Audiences were fascinated, as they were unable to comprehend the mystical powers of the hypnotist. It further goes on to commend that showmen can be quite good lay doctors.

Part one of this book describes the different parts of the show: dramatic entrance, curtain rising, stage setting described, appearance of performer, opening speech, committee invited on stage, electrical apparatus, exhibition of electrical apparatus, cures previously effected, cure of patients, hypnotic experiments, and the finale. It should be remembered again that the definitions of a medic, surgeon, dentist, barber and showman that we have today were less defined then.

The second part of the book illustrates how stage hypnosis and electricity can cure members of the audience of ills and ailments, treating paralysis and many other conditions that had supposedly been unaffected by ordinary doctors. The would-be stage hypnotist is encouraged to hold a midday consultation session at the theatre, prior to the performance, to select which volunteers could be cured. It also advises how the hypnotist can hold private sessions to cure those who have not been on the stage.

Part three of the book deals with bloodless surgery, which seems to be a form of bodily manipulation and suggestion, coupled with potions — a veritable exploitation of the illusion of the stage hypnotist's magical powers.

Part four discusses the secrets of stage hypnosis: choosing suitable subjects, preliminary tests, catalepsy, the human plank trick, breaking large stones on subjects, making horse shoes on subjects, creating sensations and other hypnotic experiences. It talks of the permanent subjects who were employed by the stage hypnotist to go up onto stage and go through the motions. These were the salaried members of the troop, who went with the hypnotist everywhere on a full-time basis. The efficacy of their successful performance encouraged the audience's belief in the hypnotist's ability.

Vaudeville Hypnotism (1930), a booklet by David J Lustic, whose stage name was La Vellma, paid great attention to the importance of colourful posters, correct placing of hoarding, dramatic build up and the right kind of opening music for the act. Indeed in his show the electrical equipment used was considered most beguiling to the audience, because many people did not have electricity in those days.

In his act an assistant was connected to the electrical equipment and then supposedly hypnotised, which apparently prevented him from being electrocuted. This gave subjects a marvellous incentive to go into trance because there was a lot of hysteria around at the time about the dangers of electricity.

Much of the act was constructed around the illusion that the hypnotist could prevent those dangers through hypnosis, and the abundance of equipment on the stage only served to enthral an already entranced audience. It is easy here to see the origins of the suggestions given by some stage hypnotists today to volunteers, that they will feel thousands of volts of electricity going through their bodies.

The booklet describes how the tradition of theatrical hypnotism prospered along with other forms of Vaudeville into the 1930s. His other books included magic, mind reading, ventriloquism, mysticism, fortune telling, crystal gazing and tricks with playing cards. The author made no pretence about his application of hypnosis for entertainment and offered various routines for sale.

His standard reproducible format, which was available by mail order, is set out as follows:

A COMPLETE TWO HOUR HYPNOTIC ENTERTAINMENT
During which time the modern wonders &

workings of the great so-and so, eminent psychologist, amuses, amazes, and astounds the natives by aid of the marvellous wonder & science of hypnotism.

Theatre Museum

Looking through the archives of the Theatre Museum in Covent Garden, London, I found a variety of material. This included a series of correspondences in 1907 about The Mystic Cavena (Frank Cavena), who billed himself as the youngest hypnotist in the world, the boy hypnotist, telepathist, personal magnet, magnetic healer, the king of scientists and the prince of fun-makers. His headed notepaper stated that he used no machinery or electricity, only pure hypnotism. There were letters offering employment to a Flo Dean asking her to work for him as his stage assistant. Flo Dean also wrote letters to the museum about her various jobs with stage hypnotists, illusionists and magicians, One of these detailed a very nasty incident in Belfast when the audience did not believe that the act was genuine and a riot commenced, causing the manager to close down the theatre.

Another piece of correspondence from the same period was from Ahrensmeyer, The Cowboy Hypnotist, who was also known as The Wizard of the Plains. His communication spoke of the marvellous "stone-breaking test", which consisted of a woman hypnotised in full view of the audience, her pulse accelerating to 126 per minute in the space of 20 seconds. Her body was rendered as rigid as an iron girder and she was suspended on the backs of two chairs, her ankles resting on one and her shoulders resting on the other.

Then a block of Portland stone measuring 24" x 25" x 8" was placed on her body and broken with a 14lb sledge hammer. Qualified medical men were invited onto the stage during the performance of this test to satisfy themselves that it was genuine. The block of stone was also open for examination for its soundness.

Another part of his performance was "the sleeping lady", who was on view in the hall of the theatre, hypnotised at

11.30am every Tuesday to Friday each week and awak-ened every evening during the performance.

Ahrensmayer also performed "the blindfolded drive through the street by route previously traversed by a com-mittee of gentlemen well-known locally and pressman". This act of extremely accurate photographic memory and co-ordination is the kind of technique we use in modern times in accelerated learning and PhotoReading.

One of his publicity stunts was the daily curing of crip-ples, paralytics, rheumatic and neurotic subjects, free of charge. This is the same kind of offer that is made by mod-ern-day stage hypnotists and no doubt they do help some of their subjects, but they do this without sufficient train-ing in any of the healing professions. Such parsimonious benevolence is often part of the stage hypnotist's publicity campaign and is designed to make them appear more qualified and endowed with abilities than they actually are. Unfortunately many of these free cures are subject to a high failure rate, often sabotaging the subjects' chances of further professional help.

A Henry Fellows wrote to the *Times* on 27th December 1951, calling for a total and complete ban on hypnosis for entertainment purposes, saying how the medical profes-sion had been calling for its use to be restricted to medical use only, for over 150 years

British Hypnotism Act 1952
A magazine report (title unknown) from 14th April 1953 talked about the new British Hypnotism Act that had been implemented on 1st April of that year. This came about because the stage hypnotist Ralph Slater appeared in court in Brighton in 1948 when one of his stage volun-teers, who he had hypnotised, sued him for assault and professional negligence. The plaintiff was awarded dam-ages. An appeal was later allowed on the issue of negi-gence, but dismissed on the issue of assault. This case drew the attention of the public and authorities to the need for legal guidelines and controls.

After much deliberation the British Hypnotism Act 1952,

which contained measures on regulating stage hypnosis for entertainment, was brought through by a private members bill. It was placed on the statute book, with a requirement for the minimum age for volunteers to be 21. However, because none of the local authorities responsible for policing the bill understood or knew how to interpret it, it proved virtually useless. Stage hypnotists continued to damage and abuse their subjects with little concern or understanding of the long-term consequences of their actions.

The article further reported that hypnotism for entertainment had been banned in Switzerland, Holland and Belgium in the early 1890s.

The *Daily Express* reported how the 150 members of the London County Council had taken three minutes, on 3rd March 1953, to ban stage hypnosis from London altogether. It further went on to say how Dr Hastings, who had piloted the new Hypnotism Act in 1952, was very angry because it had been watered down as it went through the House of Commons.

Dr. Hastings, commented on the LCC's decision: "I am overjoyed with the bold step taken by the council. I hope more local authorities will follow this lead."

I found a clipping from a newspaper of unknown origin dated around 1976, which contained an article written by John Falding, in a subsection called Night Life. He wrote about a stage hypnotist called Edwin Heath, who was performing at the New Cresta Cabaret Restaurant in Solihull and who billed himself as the world's foremost hypnotist. The act had been suspended by the local magistrates because it was being performed without the appropriate entertainment licence. Heath saw fit to point out to the reporter that he was also a member of the Belfast Branch of the Society for the Advancement of Clinical Sciences, and said that he often gave lectures to doctors and dentists.

In 1978 the *Daily Telegraph* carried a story about the stage hypnotist Malcolm Potts, who was fined £25, plus £20 costs for performing stage hypnosis without a music and dancing licence. The maximum fine for such an offence was £50. The show had taken place at a public house in Penzance and the local policeman had been tipped off in advance that it was going to happen, but he ended up being dragged into the show, in full uniform, to play a fairy godmother.

The *Times* in 1987 carried an article on 25-year-old Andrew Newton, a stage hypnotist who was allowed to break the London ban on stage hypnosis by being granted a licence to perform at the Wyndhams Theatre. Apparently Westminster Council officials had seen the act in Folkestone and loved it. Afterwards they ignored the previously ruling and allowed him to perform an initial 14 performances in the West End.

Objections came from Dr David Waxman, a past president of the British Society of Medical and Dental Hypnosis. He warned of the dangers of stage hypnosis and called for it to be banned totally throughout the country.

In the *Sunday Telegraph* in 1994 Newton said he had taught himself hypnosis from books and practised on his friends. He said: "I want to be a millionaire so badly I can almost taste it." When asked what he would do after he had made his first million, he said he would make another. His recipe for being a successful stage hypnotist was having only 25% knowledge; the other 75%, he claimed, was practice.

In 1991 the *Times* ran an article about stage hypnotists, including the antics of Peter Powers, self-confessed "naughty" stage hypnotist, who had been invited to perform at an annual corporate event. The reporter commented that much alcohol had been consumed before the performance began. Among Powers's routines was one where he had his male subjects experiencing the pain of childbirth and it seemed that their cries were surprisingly real. One subject was confused and upset when he found himself with the belief that he had given birth to an alien from another planet. The finale consisted of all the subjects performing a striptease.

The Manchester Evening News, in 1995, also ran an article on Powers, reporting an accident which happened on his tour in Australia. Apparently while doing a show in a nightclub he hypnotised a man, suggesting to him that he was James Bond. The subject consequently blew off his thumb with a starting gun and Powers described it as looking like a "burst sausage". Fortunately surgeons were able to sew the thumb back on and Powers was released without being charged.

A large article appeared in the *Independent* in 1995, recalling the career of Peter Casson (1921-1995), the famous English stage hypnotist. It recounted how in 1952 the BBC tried to record his stage show at the Alexandra Palace studio, but ran into problems when several of the crew went into trance. Afraid that Casson would have viewers all over Britain going into trance too, the project was abandoned. He did, however, continue to fill 2000-seat theatres all over the country.

After a worldwide tour Casson ended up heading the bill at the London Palladium. While the article said that he went on to lecture to psychotherapists and other clinicians, it neglected to mention that he was not accepted by the medical and psychological professions due to their general prohibition on hypnosis for entertainment purposes. With the fall in the popularity of variety theatre and the rise of television, Casson built his own nightclub in Barnsley where he was able to continue his career. He was still going strong at 70, performing to wide audiences.

It was Casson who formed the British organisation, which called itself the Federation of Ethical Stage Hypnotists (FESH), although it has never been officially recognised by any government or caring profession body. He was reported as saying that he would not let many of the rising stage hypnotists into the federation, because the standard of their acts left a great deal to be desired. In one statement he said that although there were only 25 members of FESH he believed that the number of cowboy acts reached into the hundreds and maybe thousands. He suggested that there should be an official register, but the different aspects of the caring profession were unable to sanction this viewpoint in any way.

A very comprehensive article by Susannah Herbert appeared in *The Sunday Telegraph* in 1991, which profiled the acrimony among Britain's stage hypnotists. It opened with a description of the scene at the Royal Opera House in Scarborough where stage hypnotist Ken Webster's two male subjects were running around the stage nearly naked, and as they dropped to the floor and into trance on his command of **SLEEP**, he warned them to get up in case they had homosexuals after them.

Herbert said that this was far tamer than the kind of show that first put Webster under the spotlight two years earlier at Yarmouth, where he had volunteers simulating sex with rubber dolls and imaginary sheep.

The article explained how, that summer, Britain's stage hypnotists were at war with each other. There were stories of sabotaged shows, stolen routines and defaced posters. The impresario Peter Jay was quoted as saying that he had never known performers hate each other more.

It seems that four years earlier the spilt had occurred when Peter Casson, the founder of FESH, and other stage hypnotists had battled for the ratings and star billings. The revolt had been led by Webster who formed the British Council For Professional Stage Hypnotists. Then it seemed the rival council had their own internal battles and split into factions.

In the article Webster said that sabotage and threats were common and explained how he had other people's posters stuck over his own, menacing telephone calls, stooges planted in his audiences to wreck his show, and even heavies sent in. When we consider that one show could make the performer thousands and even tens of thousand of pounds, it is not hard to see the motivation for these battles.

The article went on to say that all stage hypnotists knew the dangers and pitfalls, and Webster admitted having had one subject go into an epileptic fit during a performance. He saw hypnotism as a bit of fun and when asked about the welfare of the subjects, who had taken their clothes off during the show, he replied: "Flipping dickheads. That's what they are."

In 1994 Chris Brooke, a *Daily Mail* reporter went to study with the stage hypnotist Delavar, who was president of the British Council of Professional Stage Hypnotists. Delavar, whose real name was Gordon Mee, told the reporter that learning to hypnotise someone was really very simple. Within two hours Brooke said he had eight young women at The Lucie Clayton Secretarial School in Kensington eating out of his hand.

Delavar had told him that there was no danger in hypnosis itself, only from inexperienced hypnotists. He seemed to think that uncancelled post-hypnotic suggestions were the main cause of the problems. Even though he had been practising as a stage hypnotist for 60 years, there was no mention in the article of him having had any kind of formal training or qualifications.

In August 1997 the *Daily Telegraph* reviewed the appearance of the Australian stage hypnotist Shane St James, son of the stage hypnotist Martin St James, at the Edinburgh Festival. One of the reviewers, Kate Bassett, found the show so disturbing she burst into tears and reported that she thought that St James humiliated people in the name of entertainment. She described him as "a nasty piece of work" who created the most ethically provocative show she had ever seen at the festival.

The BBC archives
One of the problems of researching the representation of stage hypnosis on television is that the majority of commercial television stations either do not have archives or have very minimalist representations of their broadcasts. So, my research in this area was restricted to the BBC.

I believe the televising of stage hypnosis may have taken place in America and other countries earlier than in England, around the 1950s; however, since I am British and living in England when writing this work, I must hold my hands up and confess some ignorance. There is the added problem that many of the broadcasts of the early years went out live and were unrecorded and many of those that were recorded have been lost. Others were on film and have either decayed, been lost or have been expunged to make room for the companies' higher prioritised needs.

The BBC started up again after the Second World War and its library section was formed in 1948. There are records of programmes on the healing and scientific uses of hypnosis from 1950 onwards, but no reference to hypnosis as a form of entertainment until 1967. As mentioned earlier the filming of Peter Casson's hypnotic show at the Crystal Palace studio in the 1950s was abandoned and never televised.

In July 1967 the *Horizon* series featured a special edition on hypnosis and its applications. The majority of the programme considered the clinical and experimental uses of hypnosis, but a section was included on stage hypnosis and the dangers that could arise from such performances. It showed a stage hypnotist giving a demonstration of the human plank trick, with a man's body suspended between two chairs while two men jumped up and down on him.

Further comments were made about how it was the mysticism and black magic illusions that surrounded stage hypnosis which caused the public to be afraid when it was suggested for medical or therapeutic uses. One of the conclusions of this programme was that it was a powerful commodity and could be very dangerous in unscrupulous hands.

In the 1970s the *Man Alive* programme reviewed the uses and abuses of hypnosis. The crew went to a club in High Wycombe to film the stage hypnotist Martin St James, whose subjects were put through some of the standard entertainment routines of pretending to be typewriters, washing machines and snake dancers. He also demonstrated the 11 fingers illusion routine with a young woman, who, while in trance, developed a belief that she had another finger. His argument against his critics was that he thought hypnosis was a science of consent and people would not go into trance unless they wanted to.

In an interview he said that those who make the laws do

not really understand hypnosis. He admitted that he had hypnotised over 100,000 people and had three accidents, which he said were bound to happen from time to time.

Professor Desmond Ferneaux, who was a research psychologist from Brunel University, also appeared on the programme as a guest speaker. He stated that he believed that people could be made to do things against their normal moral or behavioural code while under hypnosis. His explanation for this was that by creating an altered, hallucinated reality, the hypnotist then caused the subject to change their own model of the world and different relevant moral or behavioural codes could come into play.

Another guest was Peter Blythe, a psychologist, who objected to hypnosis being used on stage. He stated that he had witnessed a case of a subject who had gone into a psychotic episode because of stage hypnosis. The subject had been told he was in contact with aliens from Mars. After the show the subject could not understand how the hypnotist had known that he had been talking to Martians for over 20 years.

In the 1980s Russell Harty, the chat show host, decided to feature the stage hypnotist Andrew Newton on his show. Selected members of the audience had been hypnotised off stage before the show and on cue 10 hypnotised subjects were seated on the stage demonstrating the imitation of musicians' routine, seeing the audience naked through special glasses routine, shouting like a sergeant major, eating onions in the belief they were apples and, of course, the standard imaginary striptease artist routine.

British television saw the arrival of the stage hypnotist Paul McKenna in the 1990s, who, backed by the prestigious promoter Harvey Goldsmith, was able to make inroads into television entertainment like no other stage hypnotist had ever done before.

In 1994 the Kilroy programme had an audience participation debate which looked at the issue of people being damaged by stage hypnosis. This was screened the week after the British government announced a review of the laws on this form of entertainment.

A woman called Kathy Nickson spoke about her night of horror when she and her husband were hypnotised in a nightclub against their will. Very disturbed, her husband became violent and she was told that she had a different identity other than her own. She described the problems that began when they arrived home and her husband performed the whole show over again in front of her children. At her wit's end and unable to control the situation she eventually called an ambulance.

According to Nickson, one of the suggestions that the stage hypnotist had given to her husband was that when his head hit the pillow he would make love to anything 50 times better than he ever had before. Injured and distressed, her husband was eventually committed to a mental hospital

Consultant psychiatrist Dr Tom Travellyan spoke of the dangers of stage hypnosis and how he thought the stage hypnotists got out of bearing responsibility by saying that people hypnotise themselves. The audience, which included several people who had been damaged by stage hypnosis, seemed very angry that such performances were allowed.

Peter Casson, president of FESH, was on the show, along with other stage hypnotists. At one point the whole show turned into a slanging match between the stage hypnotists themselves as they argued out which one among them was qualified and which was not. A representative from the Royal College of Medicine pointed out that none of them had what he thought was a qualification between them.

Another young man explained how, in Gibraltar, he had been told by a stage hypnotist during a show, that he had lost his brain. Afterwards, never having been ill before, he went into two years of manic depression, lost his job, his relationship and became an alcoholic.

For over 200 years now hypnosis has moved in and out of popularity, for the most part being used by doctors, dentists, hypnotherapists, psychologists, psychiatrists and pastoral counselling. More recently it has been used in education to stimulate and fine tune learning abilities. Stage hypnosis for entertainment has only been a tiny part of its use and always a controversial one, with the caring professions constantly warning against the dangers.

From hypnosis being in the hands of a few priests used for exorcism, it has come to be public property, revered for its ability to produce therapeutic cures and its apparent entertainment miracles.

There is no doubt that hypnosis has been a very powerful medium in influencing the thoughts and behaviours of our time, both in its minimalist use as a clinical and mental paradigm, and in its use as an expansionist concept of communication. It has once again become very popular and influential today, as it was in ancient cultures.

The most popular use of stage hypnosis was probably in the variety theatres from the beginning of Vaudeville onwards. Records of such performances are, unfortunately, patchy and little evidence has been left behind of its existence, either as memorabilia or in documented form. The evidence of its popularity at that time only arises from a few poorly preserved pieces of information.

However, over the last 20 years stage hypnosis has taken an upturn again with its eventual arrival on television in the game show format, fitting into light entertainment spots. Commercial television in the late 1990s is becoming ever increasingly competitive with the emergence of thousands of television channels all over the world. The war of the ratings and revenue leads the television companies to flaunt previously held notions of permissible entertainment and they plummet for sensationalism in the name of profit and viewing figures.

The most prestigious of television channels can screen an investigative programme on the dangers of stage hypnosis and then turn about face by putting the very same kind of show on, in order to increase viewing. I suppose had television been around 200 years ago we would have had Friday night viewing at the guillotine.

Commercialism reigns - another day another £ or $.

Stage hypnosis on television is the latest development that will inevitably run its course until the public get bored with it and a new craze hits the screens. Meanwhile theatres and other entertainment venues continue to book stage hypnotists as they draw large crowds and generate revenue. Historically it seems the shows go on, unless stage hypnosis for entertainment is legally prohibited

5

Telling It Like It Was

In this chapter are statements made by those who have suffered side effects after having taken part as subjects in stage hypnosis shows. Nothing has been altered, edited or doctored. These people compiled their own stories and were not influenced by me or anyone else. I believe it is one of the truest scientific methods possible to assess human experience by considering a person's interpretation of their own experiences; in this way we can learn a great deal. Each person's identity has been changed in order to protect their right to privacy.

To allow a person's own subjective accounts of events is to consider that experience through their perceptions

Stephen

About nine years ago I went out to see a show in the private club at my local hospital. A stage hypnotist had been arranged to entertain people. I was pushed out into the middle of the floor and told to sit in the chair. I was not warned of any type of danger.

I thought that I could never be hypnotised by anyone, but I was hypnotised and I was under for about two hours. I was doing all sort of things like being a ballerina, a dog chasing a cat and arguing over a fence with my neighbour next door. I was the star of the show, the people told me after the hypnotist had brought me around.

For the next two weeks I was having very bad headaches. Then, all of a sudden I had a nervous breakdown. I vanished for two days with my small son, and my wife had the police out looking for me. I lost my job that I had in the hospital and I have never worked since. I was put on medication for severe depression, which I am still taking, nine years later.

The government should put a stop to the cowboys that go around pubs and clubs hypnotising people just for the fun and money. They do not understand the damage they are doing to people's minds.

Elizabeth

In 1994 I booked a stage hypnotist show at the local football and social club. I volunteered to take part in the show. There was a hand clasp test done on the audience, then about six or seven of us were selected but five could not be hypnotised, which left two of us to do the show.

I was put under hypnosis at 9.15pm. I know the time because the green light which I followed was directly in front of the clock. We were asked to do various silly pranks and I was brought out of hypnosis at 11.15pm, but was still following the hypnotic suggestions eg "looking for my boobs", "couldn't leave the room because I was given an electric shock at the exit". The hypnotist then sat with my guests and he was showing everyone how susceptible I was by giving me more hypnotic instructions, like making me believe I was in love with him.

The hypnotist finally brought me out of my trance at about 11.45pm. I felt very strange — I was in a daze, my head was pounding, the room was spinning and I felt as if I was floating. My husband brought me home and put me to bed. The room was spinning, I felt utterly exhausted but I was afraid to go to sleep. I was terrified of lying down so I sat up all night. I had tunnel vision and my head felt like it was going to explode. There was no tablets that would take it away.

I was like this for about three or four days when I decided to see my doctor, who gave me a thorough examination and told me I was suffering from post-hypnotic trauma. He explained that when something stresses you a chemical is released from the brain, which causes all these ill feelings. He asked me to see him the following week. I couldn't walk in a straight line, I became very distant, still suffering the tennis ball sensation in my head, anxiety attacks, and I had to stop driving. I had no concentration.

When I did have to go out, it got so that I couldn't hold a conversation and people asked if I was drunk or on drugs. I was on no medication at that time, nor did I drink any alcohol.

We tried to contact the hypnotist, but his agent told us that he was on tour in Germany. He rang me when he got back in April. I was still a zombie. He asked me how I felt and told me not to worry. He said I was very susceptible and he agreed I was traumatised. He told me not to worry and that he would pay all my expenses for me to see a hypnotherapist. I told him that the doctor had prescribed Prozac for me so I would try these first. I was still terrified of hypnosis.

After I had been on Prozac for 10 days I felt a little better and my headaches were not quite so bad. I still suffered anxiety attacks and sleepless nights but slept all day. I had no energy, no concentration, and still couldn't hold a conversation. I became very nasty with my husband and seven children. I just couldn't cope with life anymore.

My doctor did not know what to do with me. He sent me for lots of blood tests for various illnesses. He told me I was suffering from depression but assured me he would make me better. I told him the hypnotist had offered to pay for me to see a hypnotherapist, but my doctor was very wary of me being hypnotised. He told me I had been foolish for going on stage and, in his own words, "I would never let anyone take control of my brain", so I decided to carry on with Prozac, but I did not get well with the tablets.

Eventually I was sleeping 16 hours a day. I had put my two-year-old daughter in full-time playgroup as I couldn't look after her. I got so down I tried to commit suicide twice. I told my husband I had tried to run my car into a tree and that was the turning point for me. I went and told my doctor about the suicide attempts and I told him I would not take any more tablets.

This all happened a year ago. I still don't feel back to my old self. I used to be very energetic: I did sports four times a week, I used to run a voluntary youth club, I arranged social events and fund-raising evenings for my youth club besides being a mum to seven children. I was also my husband's business partner in his painting and decorating business.

Now I do nothing. I find life very difficult and very bleak sometimes. I know I am getting better through the loyal, solid support of my husband and children, but it is an uphill struggle. My family have been to hell and back living with me these past 12 months. I am sick and tired of hearing stage hypnotists deny they do any damage and I now feel strong enough to do something about it. Stage hypnotism must be banned.

During my research I was able to see a doctor's report on Elizabeth, which confirmed that she was still suffering from post-hypnotic trauma, lethargy and depression six months after the show.

Elizabeth's In-laws

My wife and I are the parents-in-law of Elizabeth. We visited my son Ron and his wife Elizabeth and family on the day following the stage hypnosis show, which had been held at the local football and social club. At this time we were not aware that Elizabeth had been hypnotised.

It was immediately obvious to us that she was far from well. She was complaining of pains in the head and neck, appearing to have difficulty concentrating in the general conversation taking place.

We were then told about the hypnosis, which had been carried out on the previous night. My son Ron was naturally quite worried about his wife's condition but we all assumed that this would wear off and Elizabeth would be back to her normal self very quickly. We have since realised how wrong our assumptions were.

As a young mother of seven children, Elizabeth had, in the past, found time and energy for swimming, dancing, keep-fit, and playing for a rounders team. She also, along with her husband, organised a youth club and various social functions at their football club.

In the 13 months since the stage hypnosis show we have seen our previously full-of-life daughter-in-law having to gradually give up these activities. During last summer she had periods of becoming quite lethargic and she has admitted having periods of severe depression along with mood swings.

Elizabeth has visited her doctor regularly during this period and various tests have been carried out. The Prozac treatment which was prescribed has helped her very little. There have been occasions when the situation seemed to be resolving itself but these have only been temporary improvements.

The love and support of her husband and family during this difficult time have always been there for Elizabeth. We are all hoping that some time soon she will again be the vibrant, energetic young woman she was before she was hypnotised at what was intended to be a fun night out.

Elizabeth eventually issued proceedings against the stage hypnotist involved, who, after more than five extensions, did not enter a defence into the court. The case was therefore won by default and the county court ruled that it was proved, in March 1997, that Elizabeth suffered psychological damage. We believe that the defendant was unable to come up with any experts witnesses who would speak on his behalf. At the time of press financial damages were being assessed.

Elizabeth's Friend

About 18 months ago I went to a stage hypnosis show that my friend Elizabeth had organised. I attended with some reluctance because I had been to another show some time before and I did not like it. I had been a volunteer on the first occasion and have suffered side effects ever since and the only reason I attended this show was because Elizabeth was trying to raise money for her youth club she ran at that time.

The hypnotist asked whether any of us had been to a show and been hypnotised before, so I raised my hand and he asked me to go on stage. I did not want to but because of the pressure being put on me as a party pooper, I went. I asked him not to put me under as I was afraid but before I knew it I was on the floor. I was angry and told him to get me up, which he did.

I went back to my seat and when the show started I was fine, but as it went on I found I was unable to keep myself awake. I also found I was following the instructions he was giving to his volunteers (much to the enjoyment of the people around me).

When the show finished my friend John asked me if I was ok but I was far from fine; I could not bring myself round to a state of normality. My friend called the hypnotist over and he sat with me and asked me to count down from the number 10 to 0. He told me I would be fine. Since then I have had feelings of tiredness coming over me at certain times of the day. Also the most worrying symptom is that I have developed the shakes. It seems that when I get involved in a good conversation, where I have to participate fully, my stomach churns and my hands and body shake badly. It seems that my body will only let me get to a certain level before it has a cut-off valve. So now I just listen and answer in short sentences to keep the shakes away.

Also I find when I am driving (this is when I notice it more), my eyes go into a stare and I cannot blink, seeming to go into a trance, but I am aware of my surroundings. These changes have only occured since I was hypnotised. The shakes are always followed by headaches and dizzy spells. I get a feeling of light headedness too.

The same night I watched my friend Elizabeth on the stage and we were all worried about her as she seemed to be in a constant state of sleep and she did not respond with as much enthusiasm as the other volunteers. Of course I was affected myself during the show, even though I was back in the audience, but my friends were very worried about Elizabeth.

Stage hypnosis is dangerous if it can affect the audience, which it has, so therefore it cannot be regulated. I believe stage hypnosis should be banned.

Julia

While at a famous holiday camp on a Saturday night, a stage hypnotist came on stage. I went up onto the stage along with some more people, thinking that I would be there for five minutes or so, but it lasted more than an hour. When I came off I felt weird, and when I went back to my seat I could not find my husband or my friends, so I panicked, thinking I had done something which had embarrassed them, causing them to leave in disgust.

When my husband came back I burst into tears. He said I had done nothing to upset anyone. I was confused and did not know what I had done. All I could remember is going on stage and coming off again. They brought the stage hypnotist back to see me, who put me under again, but I still could not remember anything.

The stage hypnotist asked if I wanted to remember so that "when your friends talk to you, you will understand what they are saying". He put me under for a third time, but I still could not remember anything.

I said to my husband: "Let's go back to the chalet" and I went to bed. During the night I heard my husband saying: "It's all right, you've been dreaming." I was shaking like I was having a fit. I went to the toilet and found blood on my face. I must have had a nosebleed. I did not feel well and started to vomit, bringing blood up. I felt dizzy and weird but went back to bed.

In the morning my husband made me a coffee and then I started to vomit, again bringing up blood. Later I went for a walk for some fresh air to the main complex. I was feeling hot and not well at all. I felt sick and went to the toilet, still bringing up blood. I saw a friend of my husband, and asked him to let my husband know I was going for a walk to try and get some fresh air.

Afterwards I went to meet my husband, who bought me a coffee but after I took one sip I wanted to be sick again, so I went to the toilet. I must have passed out as all I can remember is a nurse talking to me and telling me I had been sick and was bringing up blood. I also felt hot and cold, could not breathe properly, and everything looked blurred. The nurse said she would arrange for a doctor to see me, and called an ambulance. I can't remember much then until I came around in hospital with a nurse telling me they were carrying out tests.

I could not see what the nurse was doing but I was asked to give a sample of urine and they gave me an eye test. I also had pains in my stomach and my back was hurting. They told me I had a water infection and that the blurred vision may be connected to the stage hypnosis, but it would clear soon.

I was given a course of antibiotics, some painkillers and discharged, being told to contact my own doctor if I had not improved. On the way back home I fell asleep for about 20 minutes. When I woke up I could just about see the outline of my husband, but not clearly. I could not eat or drink anything as I kept bringing everything back up. I spent a restless night in bed.

Monday morning my husband left me in bed and took the children to school. When they had gone I got up to go to the toilet and the next thing I know I was being woken up again by my husband. I was lying face down on the floor and could not remember how I had got there. When I got up off the floor he saw that I had a cut on my forehead, above the eye, where I had fallen and he took me to hospital.

They gave me a thorough examination and sent me for an X-ray. I still could not see properly, just like on the Sunday. The doctor said my blurred vision could be connected to the stage hypnosis, but should clear up after a good night's rest. He said I should go home and have a complete rest and drink two jugs of water before bedtime to clear the infection.

I went home and settled down on the settee. I took a painkiller with water but brought it straight back up again. I could not eat or drink anything for the rest of the day. My husband went to work at 4.00pm and I must have fallen asleep because I woke to see the children using the telephone. They had rung my husband at work to say I was ill. I started to talk to him but the receiver dropped out of my hand.

The next thing I knew, John had come home from work. He helped me to bed, and the following day, Tuesday, I still could not eat or drink until the evening when I took a pill with some cordial. I was all right and slowly started to eat and drink again. My husband went back to work again on the Wednesday.

Parts of me want to remember what happened, but other parts of me want to forget.

Emily

I am becoming more and more concerned about the public's growing interest in hypnosis as "fun" and an acceptable form of entertainment, without any realisation of the aftermath. To give you some idea of the trauma the "fun" can produce, I'd like to relate my experience of being hypnotised by a stage hypnotist. You will see how and why my attitude towards this idea of hypnosis as a form of entertainment has changed. I know I am not alone in these feelings.

The following happened during the time we lived in Germany, between 1983-84 and took place at an army barracks, in the mess. The entertainment was a disco and the hypnotist. It must have been a formal function because I remember I wore a long dress.

The hypnotist began by asking everybody to interlock their fingers and raise their arms above their heads. I joined in the "fun" and duly followed his instructions. He then asked us to see if we could pull our hands apart. I couldn't and he asked me to come forward so he could unlock my fingers. I don't remember how he freed my hands.

He next asked me to look into his eyes and I recall thinking what evil eyes he had. He asked me to lock my knees and I remember him saying: "When you wake up you won't be able to move."

Then I remember him inviting me to "come over here",

or some other encouragement to move. I laughed because I couldn't move my legs and my knee would not bend to enable me to walk. I can remember thinking that hypnosis really does work, that it is not staged or acted, because it really was happening to me.

I next recall being told that when I sat down the seat would be wet. I remember looking at the seat of the chair, but not knowing why or what I was checking. I then sat down and was aware that the hypnotist was talking, but not what he was saying, although I knew he was not talking to me. Then for some reason I felt compelled to stand up and re-check the seat of the chair. I stood up to look at it, touched the seat, and then sat back down again.

I then found myself standing up again, touching the seat of the chair and also the back of my dress. The hypnotist asked me what was the matter and without thinking I found myself saying that the seat was wet. But I also remember feeling confused because I couldn't see any liquid on the seat and my dress was dry. He then suggested that I sat on another seat, which I did.

I cannot remember in which order the next three things happened:

1. I remember being told that all the men in the room were not wearing any trousers and that I would find it very funny. I recall being asked to look at a man who was sitting directly in front of me, but was not part of the act. I immediately focused on his legs and remember smiling. I also looked at the DJ's legs and remember trying to hide a laugh behind my hand and shaking my head.

Everywhere I looked I only seemed to see men, no females at all. I honed in on their trousers and remember feeling amused by all the legs and trying to politely hide this amusement. But I certainly remember that they were all properly dressed, but still I couldn't help looking at their legs and laughing.

2. I was sitting down again when I heard the hypnotist telling somebody else they could speak moon language. I remember thinking: "Oh I could do that!" He was saying something about it not always working for everybody. I found my self standing beside a man and we were both talking gobble-de-gook conversation into the microphone. He spoke to me in this gobble-de-gook way but I just shook my head. I can never remember jokes and even if I had thought of one, the sergeants' mess was hardly the place for me to tell it.

3. The hypnotist told everyone that I would find him very attractive. I remember watching him while he was talking to the audience and to my horror he caught me admiring him. He asked me if everything was all right and I nodded my head, still unable to take my eyes off him. Then I caught a glimpse of my husband and I remember thinking: "Crickey, he's seen me in another person's arms."

I didn't seem to be able to alter the situation, so I turned my head away. I remember thinking if my husband doesn't see my face then he might not realise it's me. The hypnotist asked if everything was all right and I said: "My husband is there." I felt hurt and embarrassed when he told everyone what I had just said.

The very last part was when another lady and I were both told that we had each lost a breast. Then the hypnotist thanked us for taking part and sent us back to our seats.

As I went back I found myself discreetly looking under the chairs and tables on both sides of the room. I knew I had to search but I did not want to bring attention to myself. I reached my husband and asked him to help me search. He asked me what I was looking for and I did not want to tell him but I needed help so I braced myself and heard myself whisper that I had just lost a breast. He said (in what seemed an overtly loud voice) "What? I didn't hear you".

Again I whispered to him and moved off to resume searching. Then I realised that my husband had not moved. I pleaded with him to help me look but he just laughed. I moved away feeling totally betrayed by him. I could not understand why he was being so unkind. I truly felt alone and began to cry. I felt so helpless.

Then somebody said: "She's crying." I next remember

being back with the hypnotist and I don't remember whether I walked to the front myself or if he came and led me. He was saying everything was all right now. He then asked me if everything was all right, and I nodded and said: "It is now." But I could not bring myself to say what had been wrong. Although I finally returned to my husband smiling, I still felt an overwhelming need to sob and sob and sob.

As I slept all through the night, the hypnotist's voice went round and round in my head, and on waking the next morning I still felt this great weight of sorrow and the need to sob.

I couldn't honestly say how long I carried this feeling and his voice around with me, but gradually his voice faded and went away. The feeling dulled but stayed in the background for over a year, until 1985, when the first lumps were detected in my breasts.

In that year I visited a mobile smear clinic back in England. The doctor asked me if I had ever examined my breasts for lumps. I said I had not and she proceeded to show me how to examine myself. To my horror she suggested that I contact my doctor because she thought she detected a lump and made an appointment for me to attend a breast clinic.

Between the initial examination and the hospital visit the hypnotist's words all came flooding back. I found it very difficult to tell my husband. I just knew he would not want me and wouldn't support me, because he had just sat there and laughed. I decided I would rather die than lose a breast.

However, I eventually told my husband and he was supportive. Although I didn't quite believe that he would maintain that support, I accepted his encouragements to keep the hospital appointments. Thank goodness I did because the lump was only a cyst, which was aspirated there and then at the hospital.

Each subsequent lump or reference to this hypnotic event brings the hypnotist's words back loud and clear, along with all the sadness and isolation. I also find myself shaking and fighting the need to go away somewhere to sob.

Dennis

In February 1993 I went to a local public house in my town with a group of my colleagues from work. We knew in advance that there was a hypnotist act on. After an hour or so the act began and the hypnotist asked for volunteers. He stressed that nobody could come to any harm. I was egged on by my friends to join in and I did.

He duly hypnotised me and we were asked to perform various acts. Some time into the act he told us that when he snapped his fingers we would feel that it was freezing cold, and that we would hold onto the person next to us really tightly to keep warm. He snapped his fingers and I held onto the chap next to me and he held onto me tightly too. He told us to squeeze each other really tightly.

I cannot remember what happened in full detail, but I remember being in some pain with the chair that I was sitting on digging into my arm. This went on for quite a while (I would say about 10 minutes) while he talked to the other volunteers and asked them to do things. I was not aware that the pain was causing me any physical damage.

Eventually he told us to stop and we did. When the man next to me let go I immediately noticed that I could not move my right hand or wrist. I still carried on with the show. I'd had a few beers and wasn't too concerned. I guessed that I had stretched a tendon and that it would recover in a bit, although one of my friends was worried and told the hypnotist.

Afterwards he asked me back on the stage and attempted to hypnotise me and told me to get my wrist to move, but this failed. I think he said it would be all right when I got out into the fresh air. We all stayed until the pub shut. I just carried on drinking with my left hand and didn't worry too much.

The next day I discovered that I still could not move my hand and this was very distressing. To look at your limp wrist and fingers and will them to move without any movement happening at all is really scary. I couldn't even lift a cigarette to my mouth. I don't know why, but I went to the pub and got drunk out of my mind. I suppose I hoped I would get better by the next day. On the second morning it was the same, so I did the sensible thing and went to the hospital. The doctor said I had a damaged nerve, and that I might never be able to move my wrist and hand again. He told me that before they could treat me I must go and see my own doctor. I went to the pub again to drown my sorrows.

The third morning I went to see my own doctor and he said that I had damaged my nerve, and it may or may not recover, depending on the extent of the damage. Then he sent me back to the hospital. There I was correctly diagnosed as having damage to my right radial nerve, leaving me unable to move my right hand, fingers and wrist. There was also numbness all the way up to the elbow.

I told the hospital doctor what had happened to me and he suggested that the damage was probably caused by excessive pressure being exerted under my armpit, as this was the root of the nerve. The best he could do was put the lower arm and wrist in plaster in order to promote recovery and stop further damage to my wrist. He asked me to return in six weeks to see if things had recovered.

During the next four to five weeks I discovered what it was like to lose the use of your right arm. For one thing I could not write and this hindered my life and was frustrating. I could not even sign my name on a cheque. My work suffered, and my love life (have you ever tried making love with a plastered arm stuck to your chest?). I could not sleep properly and the longer it went on the more afraid I became that I would never be able to move my hand again. I drank a great deal, to cover my sorrows I suppose, and to sleep. After about a month I began to suffer pain in my left shoulder, due to its now more active use.

About five weeks after the plaster was put on I cut it off with a pair of scissors in frustration. I hoped that all would be ok, but it wasn't, although I found I could move my fingers a little bit; not much but I had a ray of hope.

Things gradually improved over the next two months: slight movement of the wrist, then a bit of grip in my fingers. It was about a month later that I could pick things up, such as a cup of tea. The pain in my left shoulder persisted for about six months. It took nearly a year before I would consider that I was totally recovered (my right thumb was numb for a year).

At the time of writing this I am undergoing a voluntary nine weeks of treatment for alcoholism. It is apparent from my course of treatment that events in your life can lead to drinking problems and that this event had a significant effect on the working of my mind. I am not a great activist but I am concerned that people can volunteer for stage hypnotism without being aware that they may suffer physical or mental damage from it.

I am a chief computer programmer in a large corporation and am responsible for six highly skilled professionals, who work under me. I have worked there for 17 years, but the events of that encounter with stage hypnosis not only endangered my health but also my ability to do my job.

Patricia

While on holiday in Spain in 1995 I was hypnotised against my wishes and made to perform a stage show for approximately one hour. I had gone to a bar on a Friday night to see a hypnotist show. Volunteers were asked for and about 15 people went up onto the stage area, but I stayed in the audience.

The hypnotists, who were a man and wife team, said they were going to give a quick demonstration of the control of the mind. The audience was encouraged to hold their hands in the air and follow the hypnotists' comments and movements. We had been told to put our hands on our chins but had followed the movements and placed our hands on our cheeks.

The audience was then led into another demonstration that involved closing our eyes, clasping our hands behind our head and listening to the male hypnotist's instructions. He spoke to us for about two minutes, telling us our hands were getting glued together. We were then told, if we could, to release our hands. I could not. There were about eight of us in the audience, including myself, who were stuck and he told us if we came up to the stage he would release us.

The first person was released and sent back to their seat. The second person was put to sleep and he told her that when she heard the word "Madonna" she would shout "I am a slag" three times. He did a similar thing to a third person.

The hypnotist's wife came over to me and moved my arms over my head to the front. While she was doing this I said to her: "I don't want to do that and I don't want to be part of the show." She simply said: "Don't worry."

The hypnotist released my hands and at the same time told me, I found out later, that when I heard the word "cowboys" I would stand up and shout "the Indians are coming" three times. When it happened I was not aware of what I had said but just that I was standing in the middle of the audience and everyone was looking at me and laughing.

I found out later that he had told me that when he said the word "sleep" I would fall into a deep sleep, and this happened. The next hour is difficult to recall until the time when I went back to my seat and about three times found myself back on the stage area again.

I have been told I performed the following: ants in my pants and the desire to get them out; riding a motorbike over a bumpy road; playing a violin; hugging the person next to me to keep warm, and possibly more. One occasion when I found myself back in my seat, then back on the stage again, was when the chicken song was played and we all returned back to the stage and acted like chickens. One man was given the role of "the randy rooster" and attempted to mate with myself and other people on the stage.

Only one or two people had actually volunteered out of

the seven or eight people made to perform the show. The others were caught up by going up on the stage to have their hands freed like I was.

I am angry about the way I was trapped into performing the show, especially when I told the hypnotist's wife that I did not want to be part of it. I went to the stage believing my hands would be released and was then forced to perform the show.

I believe, very strongly, that involuntary performances must not be allowed to continue and I urge anyone to support a bill to outlaw such live stage shows.

Debby

In November 1993 I attended the show of a stage hypnotist who has performed on television, at a public function room in Gravesend, Kent. As we were seated the lights went down and the audience were told to listen carefully to what the hypnotist had to say. When the lights went down a sense of concentration filled the hall. The audience were told to close their eyes and music began to play. We were then told to clinch our fists together and hold them tightly together, as if they were glued.

My hands were very tight together and at this point they began to rise above my head. I was not sure what was happening and was not really sure how they began to rise above my head. I was also waiting for the instructions that the hypnotist was going to give out. We were then told to open our eyes and the lights came on. Everyone whose hands were above their heads were told to proceed to the stage.

After arriving on the stage we were selected down to 10 people and I still could not move my hands apart. I started to get a feeling of panic that I was not in control of my own actions. The hypnotist came towards me, placed his hand on my shoulder, then the lights appeared to me to go blue. He told me to stare at a fixed point, which was a light fitting. Music began to play and he talked into my ear with his hand on my shoulder. I felt myself drifting into subconsciousness and at this point I was not aware of anyone else apart from myself and the hypnotist.

He then moved the 10 of us onto chairs and I was not aware at this time that I had been standing there for 25 minutes. During that time he hypnotised the other nine people selected from the audience. As we were seated on the chairs I felt compelled to obey his every word. I felt a fear building up inside myself but at the same time I felt I had no choice but to do exactly what he told me to do. There were various things that he told me to do, from being a washing machine or a fish, to riding a bicycle. I am a naturally bubbly person, humorous and outgoing, but I was showing no emotion at all (so I was told later) while under his influence.

He instructed us by talking to each individual on the stage, placing his hand on our right shoulders and tapping. At one point he told us that we were all compulsive liars, and this is when I felt I had lost total control of myself. I was arguing most vehemently with a total stranger and getting very emotional. I felt that it was imperative that I made my point clear.

When the interval came I was told to be a village gossip and I was left like this for 20 minutes walking around in the audience on my own. I was not aware at this juncture of who I was or where I was. I just knew that I had to speak in a country accent and talk to complete strangers. I did not even recognise my friends in the audience.

After having completed several acts for the audience there seemed to be a moment when I lost my concentration but the hypnotist would put me back into my sleep by saying "sleep". When he was bringing us out of trance, he would remind us of what we had done and I knew my eyes were closed but I was confused and felt as if I was drifting.

The whole process of bringing all 10 of us out of trance took more than five minutes and as I opened my eyes I could not believe how long I had been on the stage. It seemed like five minutes but I had actually been there for one and a half hours.

I felt immediately drained, worn out and tired. The 10 of us were each given free tickets to return to another of the hypnotist's shows and then we were all escorted from the stage. I rejoined my group of friends and they began to explain to me all the things that had taken place while I was under hypnosis. Some of them I could recall clearly but others I could not remember at all.

By the time I had reached home, approximately one and a half hours later, I had a severe headache and felt completely drained. My parents asked if I had enjoyed my evening out but I could not talk about it. All I wanted to do was go to bed because I was so very tired.

The next day I felt worn out, physically drained and still had a headache. I was questioned at work but felt reluctant to disclose what had happened to me. All I knew was that I felt very uncomfortable discussing the events of the previous evening.

The next time I felt a feeling of intense fear was when I was visiting a friend's house and the hypnotist came on the television. My first reaction was to turn the television off, as I could not bear to watch him or hear his voice. It was like a kind of fear I had not experienced before. It has now been over six months since I was hypnotised. I feel I have been very lucky not to have suffered any lasting traumas and believe that hypnosis should not be used for this kind of entertainment.

I feel that people are not aware of the anguish these kind of shows can cause the people who get hypnotised. I hope it will be banned as a form of entertainment.

Brigit

My experience happened around Christmas a few years ago. The hypnotist was present at a charity night to raise funds for a local village hall. Tickets were hard to come by and the waiting list had 40 names on it. Only by knowing a friend of the organiser did I manage to get a ticket.

The hypnotist appeared on the stage about 11.00pm, which seemed quite late at the time to me. He asked for volunteers over 18 years of age; then he told the audience that hypnosis was not dangerous and would be lots of fun. I, together with 20 other people, volunteered and went up onto the stage. He then narrowed the numbers down to 10 through various exercises, like asking us to hold an imaginary balloon filled with helium.

In the first part of the show he told me to be a reindeer and then a Christmas turkey. He also told the other girls that they had ice-cream in their hand and to lick it. This turned into a sex aid, which I found very embarrassing and offensive. Then we were told to have a 20 minute break, which we would all look forward to and in which some people were told to perform some seemingly harmless acts. We were all left alone and told there would be a big party after the break, which we would attend, on the catch words "Come and join the party".

As soon as he said those words I, along with the others, ran back to the stage, knocking both people and chairs over that got in our way. It was then that I noticed that two people were missing and later I found out that they could not carry on because they felt ill and had headaches. The organiser had not believed in the power of hypnosis and was now behind the curtain fast asleep, as he also apparently dropped out at this stage.

Then the show recommenced with the make-believe party. After the party we were told that we all had hangovers and one man ran outside and tried to make himself sick. In another stunt a man was told that he was the boxer Frank Bruno and in training for a fight. He was doing strenuous exercises when the bell rang for the fight. He fell to the floor (as he was told to do) with an almighty crash. This could obviously have done him a great deal of harm.

The men were also told to be striptease dancers and took all their clothes off apart from their underwear. The ladies were also told to be erotic dancers. Then the show ended with us all singing "Auld Lang Syne" and the hypnotist telling us we would just remember what a good time we had. The show lasted two hours in total and it was past 1.00am when we came out of hypnosis.

As I was leaving and going to my car I felt I had a splitting headache and while driving a friend home it got progressively worse. On the way to my house I felt sick and had to have the two front windows open to keep myself from passing out. When I reached the house I staggered out of the car and managed to get to the bedroom where my boyfriend was asleep. I tried to close my eyes and sleep off the feeling but my headache was so bad I just lay there with my eyes open.

My brother fetched me some tablets, which I took, but they did not help either. My head was not just throbbing but I was in severe sharp pain all across my forehead and above my eyes. I felt only what I could describe as sea-sickness and was in tears the whole night. My brother told me that he had heard that headaches were a side effect of hypnosis because of the electrical currents in the brain.

Eventually I got a few hours sleep. The next day, a Sunday, I went to our local pub and talked to a friend who had been at the show. She told me that the organiser, who had taken part, had felt exactly the same and the owner of the local shop had to have the day off, which was a very rare occurrence. I still had the headache, although it had eased a little, perhaps due to the paracetamol.

Since then I have had a headache at least once a day, in exactly the same place, and even the doctor seems to think it was caused by the stage hypnotist's suggestions. He even offered to send me for tests. My dad was very worried because my mum had died of a brain tumour three years earlier. I had to have a week off work because of the way I was feeling and my once cast iron stomach is now very sensitive.

Altogether I am very angry and upset that these side effects occurred, because the stage hypnotist had given no indication that this could happen. I am asthmatic so my medical history had been monitored before the incident and I was all right. I wrote to my local newspaper and really believe that this kind of thing should be banned.

Rose
It was the summer of 1994 when my friend asked me if I wanted to go to see a stage hypnotist. The idea of watching

107

some guy making a fool of people for three hours didn't appeal to me. But she finally coerced me, although when I told my mum where I was going she was not very keen on the idea, as she told me these guys were cowboys and to be very careful.

My friend and I met in town and went to the show. My friend had been before and said that he was really good. When the show began he started by talking for a few minutes, saying he was in the Guinness Book of Records for putting someone into trance the fastest. He then went on to ask the audience for their concentration while they clasped their hands together and closed their eyes. As we were doing this he counted to 10 and with each number our hands were supposedly to become tighter and tighter, so much so, that they felt they had been stuck together with glue and would then shake vigorously up and down.

Well, my hands did not stick together, which was fortunate for me and I continued to watch the show. I found him very suggestive towards young girls and his actions towards his male subjects to be rough ie he would pick on one or two guys and slap them about the face and head each time he walked past them. The show went on and he targetted one or two females, whoever was wearing the least clothes or had a pretty face, and had them doing whatever he pleased. Then, after the break, in part two, was when my nightmare began.

He came and said that he needed some more people to take part in the show, so he went through the whole "hands" thing again, only this time my hands did stick together. They stuck so tightly that my knuckles went white, my hands shook tremendously and my arm muscles began to ache.

This show is pretty vague now, but my friends told me that I:

1. Seduced a tailor's dummy.
2. Went driving in my cart along a country road towards a castle then entered "The Haunted House" for a party.
3. Held the theatre walls up during an earthquake and

tried to vacate the audience.

4. Took part in the "Monster Mask" competition and several other sketches.

Before bring you out of trance the hypnotist tells you to come backstage for free tickets. And then the show ends and he asks you to return to your seats. I returned to my friends, who were hysterical with laughter as they told me of my performance. They also came with me as I went backstage to collect my tickets. I stood talking to the hypnotist for a few minutes before my friends started to call me away. The hypnotist said that I was a "good subject" before handing me my tickets. It was from that moment on that I felt the magnetism. My friends and I left to make a call for a taxi and went outside to wait for it. Outside I watched him sitting in his car before he went off.

I attended and participated in several other shows with a friend. It was after the last show in this particular season that I plucked up the courage to ask the hypnotist if I could have my picture taken with him. This happened outside the stage door of the theatre. My friend took a couple of photographs of me and him together. In these photos he has his arm around me and vice versa. He then suggested that we went inside as the lighting wouldn't be very good outside. We did and I had two or three further photos taken of us together. In one my face is as red as a tomato; whether he said something embarrassing or I had done something, I don't remember. My friend informs me that I put them in the bin after the last show.

After my friend had finished taking the photos she said: "See you outside" and I stayed to talk to the hypnotist. He said he would quite like to have one of the photos. I asked where I would send it and he then gave me his mobile phone number.

Anyway the next thing was that the hypnotist asked if he could have a kiss. I agreed but was a little reluctant, as all the stage crew were working around us. It was at this time that one of the stage crew suggested to the hypnotist that he should take me to his dressing room. I know I didn't take him up on that offer, but the last memory I have is of him asking me to call him when I got the photos developed.

It was after each show that I saw a pattern developing. After getting home I was physically sick, had diarrhoea and suffered abdominal cramps. At one show I received some bumps and bruises to my head and arms. Also I began suffering some terrible headaches, which, at the time, I did not relate to hypnotism until I started to attend appointments with the doctor. He looked into several avenues as these headaches were occurring every day. My doctor referred me to an optician, who, after various examinations, told me that my prescription had not changed since my last eye examination. So after various investigations my doctor asked if I had taken part in stage hypnotism at any point.

Bingo! We had now found the reason for several ailments: constant lethargy, nausea, irritability, mood swings, and unexplained personality changes. I had taken several friends to these shows and had exhausted them all.

One evening my mum asked to come along to see what the big deal with this hypnotist was. Well, she was disgusted at this so-called "family show" where young men stripped off to their boxer shorts, thinking they were strippers and some of them took the lot off.

Now let me explain the last show — I can't really remember the date. What I do remember was near the end of the show when the hypnotist had chosen me and a few others to seduce the tailor's dummy and then take part in a pornographic film. We were told that we could not see the audience, but what we could see was a screen that reflected the performances. I remember going into several different sexual positions.

We were told that whoever was the best in the film would give the hypnotist a seductive kiss. He then put us back in trance and after this, tapped my shoulder. It was me he had chosen. I opened my eyes, looked at him standing at the other side of the stage and walked up to him and gave him a big seductive kiss. He then told me to fall to my knees in front of him. Then the house lights went out. I have no recollection of what happened next. I think I remember being brought out of trance and I was lying on the stage.

While the audience roared with laughter I returned to my seat with a red, sore chin. A few guys came up to me and said: "That was some kiss." I had a very uneasy feeling about the whole thing, so much so that I never went to another one of his shows.

Now I feel I was targetted by this hypnotist and was one in a long line of magnetised females. There was another girl who hung around after the shows and on the night that I had photos taken with him, she also had some taken. One of the theatre's bouncers told me about this and said that the girl was not too happy about it. Why? Well, your guess is as good as mine.

It was magnetism that kept me going to his shows. When the hypnotist asked about these photos he also asked me out to "dinner or something", but the more I thought about it and discussed it with a close friend, the more I am glad I did not do it.

I've noticed in different newspapers over the last few years that he was performing at the theatre. Although I have felt like going I now believe it would be dangerous for me and I never want to see him again.

When I opened the newspaper last week and read about the other people who had suffered, it bought it all back to me and I decided to contact you. I had a racing mind all the time up until I fell asleep. Sometimes I thought the telephone was ringing when it was not. I feel he implanted some kind of bug in my head and I just want it out.

LETTERS TO CASH

Jill's friend

I decided to write to you to tell what happened to my friend Jill. It was a usual Saturday night and we were going out. We always had a good laugh on the weekend and some beers. My friend Jill and I worked very hard during the week. Jill wanted to go to the local nightclub to see a stage hypnotist that was performing.

We got to the nightclub and the artist came on. Well I didn't really want to see him, but I went along for Jill's sake. We were sitting at a table as he started his act. First of all he started by asking everyone in the audience to clasp their hands together. I did not because I could not be bothered to join in. It seemed a stupid act, but Jill joined in and kept on doing so. When he asked people to try and see if they could pull their hands free, Jill couldn't.

Then he asked a few people to come up on the stage (to take part in a bit of fun he said). They did the usual stupid things that go on in such shows. He also asked people to relax during his act by hearing his theme tune in their heads, and then when the show finished all the volunteers were told they were back to normal. Everyone clapped and the people left the stage.

He finished his act and Jill, who had taken part, did not seem to be quite herself. That night after the show we just thought it was one of those things and we went home. Next day Jill was supposed to come around to our house for Sunday lunch, but did not turn up. I went around to her flat and she was not well. She was still complaining of feeling dizzy and said: "Every time I try to relax I hear his theme tune in my head". It did not matter whether it was in the bath or in an easy chair.

I telephoned the nightclub and they said to bring her down to the club and they would contact the hypnotist who was at another club of theirs. He put her under hypnosis again over the telephone and said to her when she came out of trance everything would be normal.

I managed to persuade her to come around to my house and have lunch. Later that afternoon she returned to her flat, because she was really excited about going out with a date that evening, as she had liked the guy for a long time.

That afternoon another friend of ours turned up at her flat too. Jill told us she was going to wash her hair and have a bath. Little did we know that she would be slipping into unconsciousness in the bathroom. When she did not come back from the bathroom we started banging on the door. In fact we had to get a neighbour to break the door down. The police and ambulance were called because we couldn't feel a pulse. She was dead in the bath.

I blame stage hypnosis for Jill's death and I cannot be persuaded from this opinion. She was such a fun loving, happy-go-lucky and lovely person.

Hypnosis should not be used for entertainment. You don't know what you are delving into with someone's unconscious. At the inquest they said that stage hypnosis would not be allowed in the town again. I hope it is banned as a form of entertainment, because it only wrecks people's lives.

Matthew

My name is Matthew and I am 47 years of age. I used to be a happily married man and father of three girls. I was an officer in the Boy's Brigade and also enjoyed hill walking, rock climbing, sailing and camping.

Approximately nine years, a few days before Halloween, I, my wife and another couple attended a stage hypnosis show in a function room at our local bowling club in Scotland. Prior to this show my wife had always been a loving wife and mother to our three daughters. On the night of the show she was one of the volunteers who was hypnotised on the stage. She went under the spell of the hypnotist and remained under that spell for approximately one hour.

She did not make a complete fool of herself as some of the others did. She was brought out of the spell and sent back to sit in the audience with me and the other couple. She could talk to us but could not remember my name, how many children she had or their names, and after a few minutes she fell back into a trance. After the show I had to leave the hall and go to the dressing room and get the hypnotist to come out and try and help her.

This he did, after some prompting and she appeared to be back to normal. Gradually over a period of many months I found that she was suffering from depression and panic attacks. She got treatment for this from our doctor in the form of Valium and Atavan. Her attitude changed from loving to one of distrust and hatred towards me. After about three years of her putting me through agony her condition seemed to get worse and we broke up.

We divorced in 1990 but I continued to see her and eventually I moved back in with her. Things seemed to go well, although she was still suffering from depression and panic attacks, but was getting psychiatric help. Since then we have split up again, due to her accusations towards me of things I never did. I ended up in court a second time in January 1994. Fortunately I had witnesses this time to prove that her accusations were false and the case was dismissed

For someone to change from the loving wife I knew to a crazy, mixed up ex-wife, something must have caused it and it all started after the stage hypnosis. My ex-wife was a perfectly healthy, normal woman. She changed completely after that night she was hypnotised and I believe this was to blame for her condition. It has ruined my life, our family's lives and her own. She became a different person after the show and has never been the same since.

All stage hypnosis must be banned. So many people suffer after these shows and it must be stopped. In my mind it is dangerous and harmful.

Mr and Mrs Jones

I am writing with reference to our telephone conversation regarding stage hypnosis and the effects which such an experience had on our daughter. This occurrence took place last summer at the end of the university term when she went to a hypnotic show and volunteered to be hypnotised. Our daughter appeared to have been put into a hypnotic state, although she herself believed that she had not.

As the show drew to a close the volunteers were being brought out of the trance but it seemed more difficult to raise our daughter into full consciousness and she began to shake. The first thing we heard was when we got a telephone call from our daughter, who was in a distressed state. She asked us to collect her from the hall of residence because she was extremely anxious and frightened of going to sleep. We left home immediately.

When we arrived our daughter burst into tears. It was clear that being hypnotised had been a very unpleasant and frightening experience for her. Apparently the hypnotist was also concerned as he had asked her to contact him if there were any problems.

The following morning one of our daughter's friends contacted her at our house. She said that the hypnotist had contacted the hall of residence to find out how our daughter was.

Since then our daughter has refused to speak about the experience, which she obviously wants to forget and we have agreed to her wishes. She still feels this way and does not want to be personally involved in any further developments.

6

Stage Hypnosis Shows

Harry the Horny Hypnotist

Watching the trailers on a video I hired from my local rental store I came across an advertisement for a video called *Harry The Horny Hypnotist*. I then proceeded to buy it from a music store that had previously made a public statement that it would not stock it. The major theme and closing line of the trailer was: "Catch Harry the Horny Hypnotist before they do!"

The star of the video was Harry, whose carefree dressing room chats with the camera were edited into a one and a half hour stage hypnosis show, and could only be paralleled to a stand-up blue comedian. In the dressing room scenarios Harry intimately told the camera that he had not been able to get many bookings lately since a rather scandalous performance that he had given, where the newspapers had reported that he had left one of his subjects disturbed. During this interview he appeared to consume copious amounts of alcohol to bolster his confidence before he went on stage.

He said that while he was quite good at getting people into trance he had never quite mastered the art of bringing them out again. The show was recorded at a college during a students' social evening. The main theme of Harry's show was sex and his comic patter was off the cuff, base, and for a comic, very well delivered; however, his skills as a hypnotist were as far away from therapeutic as Venus is from Mars.

Having put several people into trance on the stage, he then chose one male subject and one female. He told the woman that she "shagged like a rabbit". Then he instructed her to take all her clothes off and when she was down to her suspenders and stockings she was awakened. The horrified young woman ran screaming from the club in absolute horror at finding herself almost naked. I cannot say definitely whether this young woman was actually hypnotised or just acting; she appeared to be under hypnosis and there is no reason for me to believe she was not.

Harry instructed another young woman to have the biggest and best orgasm each time he mentioned a cue word and he then practised using the word often. There would be no problem with the cue word and the orgasm technique under the right circumstances, as this could be the application of a genuine therapeutic approach. The problem arose when he then used the cue word and followed it with an aside, castigating her for it in a sarcastic manner and implying that she was of loose morals. While holding her in his arms he demonstrated the technique and the young woman had an orgasm. He then turned to the audience with a smile on his face and said: "I'm fucking good, aren't I?"

What struck me was that while under the influence of hypnosis this woman was receiving two conflicting sets of instructions that were contrary to each other. The first was for her to have an orgasm and the second message was that to do such a thing was not appropriate behaviour. There is a danger that of these two conflicting messages the second could become dominant. At some time later this woman could have feelings of wrong doing connected with sex.

As children we pick up all sorts of messages about the way we relate to our bodies and the social concepts of right or wrong concerning our sexual functions. These learnings formulate our abilities to enjoy sex, both at an unconscious and conscious level. As therapists we are able to study the people that come into our consulting rooms, who do have feelings of guilt about sex and repressed memories of being told that it was somehow wrong.

Since hypnosis is such a powerful tool, according to Harry, I am left wondering what deep unconscious learnings this young woman may have picked up from that experience and how that will affect her in the future. Certainly as a therapist I would have been struck off or sued for so carelessly implanting in the subject's mind such a set of confusing messages about a very natural function.

The young man who had been chosen to perform in the show was woken up with the suggestion that he would have the biggest testicles ever known on a human being and was then sent out to seek the assistance of the audience, who he was told were doctors. We know from the work of the American oncologists and therapists the Simontons, a man and wife team who work with cancer patients, that suggestion can have a very big effect on the induction or reduction of cancerous growths. Again, should a therapist have made this suggestion, they could have been sued and would most likely have lost the case. The same young man was then told he would fall in love and have sex with a blow-up rubber doll which was brought onto the stage.

Harry went on to perform other various skits with his subjects, including one that was a simulation of the famous Bobbit case in America. In this scene the woman is told that she has been terribly abused and hates men. In the real Bobbit case the wife cut off her husband's penis after she reported being abused by him.

The young woman was given a pair of scissors and instructed to go out into the audience where people were holding up courgettes, which she savaged with her blades. Again we are left wondering what unconscious traces this kind of induced behaviour may leave in the subject's unconscious ideation.

Hypnotists rely on the suggestions made during hypnosis to be effective and to stay with the client. This is the principle by which we seed desired behaviour, but it does not always happen that way. So why does the stage hypnotist imagine that just because they are having fun, that those suggestions will automatically totally disappear when they snap their fingers?

The finale of Harry's show came when a young woman

was instructed to strip naked and pretend she was in the shower. She was then given liberal amounts of foam to spread over her body, much to the rioting delight of the male members of the audience. At this point the police arrived, the show was stopped and Harry was handcuffed, arrested and taken away. The young woman was covered with a policeman's coat and also taken out of the hall. The students, who Harry had successfully worked up into a frenzy, were booing and shouting at the police for spoiling their entertainment.

At the end of the video it was stated that Harry was taken to court and given a six month community service order, but the real crime of mental cruelty through his reckless, incompetent use of hypnosis went completely unnoticed. As it was plain to see, the subjects were left still in trance, wandering around, confused and bewildered. The police were apparently arresting Harry for his lewd show, with possible infringement of the entertainment licence, but as they were unlikely to have had any experience of hypnosis it is possible that they may well have exacerbated any after effects or complications that those subjects may have suffered.

As to whether the events on this video were entirely true or not, I cannot guarantee, since I have taken them at face value in the way they were presented. In my opinion, the events appeared to be genuine and were typical of many live shows I have seen.

Paul McKenna

British stage hypnotist Paul McKenna is undoubtedly responsible for the upsurge in hypnosis for entertainment in the 1990s. This man has made millions of pounds from his craft in a very short space of time. His television shows have been marketed to many countries all over the world, much to the disapproval of the vast majority of professionals using hypnosis in the healthcare industries. They believe his representation of hypnosis as a quick-fix miracle cure for just about everything has done great harm to its image in the public's mind.

Mckenna, who was a disc jockey on Chiltern Radio before he learned hypnosis from books, has rocketed to fame under the guidance of the promoter Harvey Goldsmith. In one of his shows, he dubbed himself "Hypnoman" and in a television interview, *The Chair*, he described himself as a control freak who gets very stressed when he can't get what he wants.

His television shows have edited out much of the process of hypnosis, leaving what seems to be a miraculous power to control other people's behaviour.

In 1992 in the *Guardian*, McKenna declared that he had been told by psychics and astrologers that he was special. It was also reported that he believes in aura and charisma. Then the reporter said that he referred "with obvious relish" to hypnotic figures in history such as Billy Graham, Gandhi, Jesus Christ, Napoleon and Hitler.

McKenna has issued a number of lawsuits against those who have expressed criticism of his shows. Some of those lawsuits he has won, some have been settled out of court and others have not been pursued. In 1996 he issued a writ for libel against me and Michael Joseph, the owner of the *European Journal of Clinical Hypnosis*. This is covered in chapter 10 under the section entitled "The EJCH Affair".

At the time of writing this book McKenna is, of course, being sued himself. The *Daily Mail* in October 1996 reported that a 28-year-old man from London, called Christopher Gates was suing McKenna, claiming he had triggered acute schizophrenia. The complainant said that he was hearing voices from God after being hypnotised by McKenna.

After the stage hypnosis Gates regressed to childhood and wanted to play with toys all the time. It was reported that during the performance he believed he was Mick Jagger, a boy of five, an interpreter for aliens, a ballet dancer and a contestant on the Blind Date television show. Among the other things he believed that he experienced while under hypnosis were that he was walking on the moon, conducting an orchestra, on holiday sunbathing, wearing special glasses that made everyone appear naked, and riding a horse.

Gates later spent four weeks in a psychiatric hospital.

In the action it is claimed that several months later he still had to be accompanied by an adult everywhere because he thought he was eight years old. The psychiatrist in the case recommended him to the specialist hypnotherapist in this field, Derek Crussell.

This all took place at the Swan Theatre in High Wycombe in March 1994. When I spoke to Gate's girlfriend, Beverly, she said: "Our whole life has been turned upside down." This action is not expected to be tried until late 1998.

Having seen one of McKenna's stage shows at the Dominion Theatre in London in 1995, it is my opinion that he showed little regard for the welfare of his subjects. One man was told that he had lost his penis and became extremely distraught. Later that man exhibited profound signs of aggression to another subject and threatened him with violence, believing the other man had stolen his penis.

Another man was in receipt of suggestions that he should have sexual desires towards a broom. This man's penile erection was plain for all the audience to see, underneath tight fitting trousers, as he thrusted himself in the direction of the broom.

McKenna also suggested to a woman that he was her fantasy person and she appeared to become sexually excited. Yet another man was encouraged to perform mockingly as a male homosexual, while exhibiting a cataleptic arm.

An article in the *News of the World* in February 1993 reported a radio show in New York where McKenna hypnotised three women. The sound of a buzzer was used to activate the experience of the subjects having an orgasm each time the hypnotist used it. The show went out at breakfast time and was heard by millions of people and many of them telephoned in to complain about its contents. One subject who took part was very upset by the incident, saying that the very last thing she wanted was to have an orgasm in public before millions of people.

The *Daily Mirror* reported, in 1997, that McKenna had now acquired a PhD from Lasalle University in Mandeville, Louisiana, USA. When the reporter telephoned Lasalle to request a copy of the 50,000 word thesis that McKenna claimed he had written, the establishment refused to make available such information.

In order to verify this I telephoned Lasalle University myself to ask if the thesis was available for public record or inspection. However, I was told that this was not the case, unless the student wished to publish the thesis themselves. This is most odd because most universities would be extremely happy to have a thesis that they have lying on their shelves by one of their students read by anyone who was interested.

I later learnt on the internet in an article by Butch Badon of the *News Banner* in 1997, that the president of Lasalle University, Thomas Kirk, had got five years in prison and three years probation for fraud in early 1997. Part of his crimes were issuing worthless degrees that were, at the end of the day, in no way accredited, except possibly by the Big Foot examination board. Judge Martin Feldman, who heard the case, said he had administered the harshest sentence he could under the law, but if he could have given Kirk more he would have.

In an interview with the *Mail on Saturday* McKenna told a reporter that the greatest influence on his life was the works of the American psychiatrist Dr Milton Erickson. However, he failed to declare that Erickson would never have approved of McKenna's use of hypnosis because it would go against the spirit of the Hippocratic Oath. Erickson helped found the American Society of Clinical and Experimental Hypnosis, which views the use of hypnosis in entertainment as being unethical.

McKenna also set himself up as a trainer in hypnosis in 1996, running courses with the corporate trainer Michael Breen and one of the founders of Neuro-Linguistic-Programming, Richard Bandler. The certification that is offered for these courses should be dependent upon the ethical use of hypnosis if such qualifications were to be accepted by the major therapeutic organisations in England. However, an anomaly arises because in an interview with *Here's Health* magazine in 1997 McKenna declared that he would be touring in the autumn with his stage show in England and the USA. On television in the spring of 1997 he told the public they would be in for three more years of his stage shows on their screens.

His continued participation in these stage shows inevitably disqualifies him from being a trainer in the eyes of many professionals who practise hypnosis in the caring profession. Yes, he does include displays of phobia cures in some of his shows, but so have many stage hypnotists for 200 years. It is, after all, part of the publicity mechanism that stage hypnotists have exploited and the caring profession has strongly opposed.

In his book *The Hypnotic World of Paul McKenna* he says that he believes that hypnosis is undoubtedly the single most powerful resource in healthcare and personal development today. Yet in the spring of 1997 on one of his television shows he has a sketch with a young woman who has accepted the suggestion that she has lost her eyebrows.

In April 1997 in the *Evening Standard* the journalist Victor Lewis-Smith summed up many of the general public's feelings towards McKenna's shows. He talked about one of the Paul McKenna shows that was due to go out on air but was pulled because of lack of compliance to ITC broadcasting standards.

His opinion was that McKenna had made a fortune out of reviving the kind of mesmerism act on television that was tasteless and humiliating. Lewis-Smith said that McKenna would like the public to think that his work had a serious medical basis but the show he watched had nothing to do with science.

Other stage hypnotists

In Spain I saw a hypnotic stage show by an English stage hypnotist called Peter, which was held for the tourists at a resort hotel. He spent a great deal of the show bragging about how many people he had hypnotised during the summer season and the rest of the time was spent chatting to the disc jockey, not paying attention to his subjects.

At one point in the show he sent the subjects out into the audience in a deep somnambulistic state and totally ignored what they were doing while he took a bow. A large man, who was more than 20 stone in weight, was so unsteady on his feet that he fell onto two pensioners. The couple were terrified as he knocked the drinks off their table and glass went flying everywhere. Eventually waiters rescued the couple and the subject wandered elsewhere among the audience. Peter had not even noticed that this was happening because he was busy cueing the right music for his closing curtain call.

Ten fully somnambulistic subjects continued to wander among the audience, very confused and performing various repetitive tasks designed to amuse. Peter eventually told them to come out of trance and the show was over. All this was done from a microphone on the stage. They were dismissed and he took his closing bow, making no attempt to see them again or check whether they were out of the trance state or not.

The minimum age for any volunteer to have taken part in the show was 16, but I interviewed a young boy who had taken part after the show. Having lied to be picked as one of the volunteers, he admitted that he was, in fact, only 14 years old. Peter the hypnotist had not enquired about the boy's age, although it was obvious from his physical appearance that he was very young.

The shows he performed generally took place around an open swimming pool crowded with tables and drunken people. This is often the kind of environment in which many of these travelling stage hypnotists perform their shows, among waiters, sangria and chicken in the basket. I also learned that a few nights before at another location one of Peter's subjects had fallen into a swimming pool while in deep trance and had to be rescued by the staff of the venue.

I caught part of the act of another very young stage hypnotist who had been performing in the Midlands in England. This particular young man had not been practising hypnosis very long and his inexperience led him to horrify his audience. In order to entertain and appear all powerful he suggested to a young woman that when she awoke again she would believe that she had been raped.

This kind of suggestion can cause False Memory Syndrome (FMS), which, as discussed in chapter three, occurs when a person may believe that they have been physically, sexually or mentally abused, but in fact this is not the case. In cases of FMS it is the suggestion of the therapist or clinician that has caused the subject, either in hypnosis or not, to construct an artificial memory of that abuse. The subject or client truly believes that those perceived incidences of abuse took place. In therapy this can come about through the therapist's inarticulate application of analysis, looking into the past for bad experiences to explain the client's present problems. Particularly in psychoanalysis, it is believed that memories from the past cause present problems. The constant and sometimes chronic digging for those memories can cause the patient to create FMS to satisfy the therapist.

The stage hypnotist considers none of these dynamics when making suggestions to the subject's unconscious mind. When the woman awoke and believed she had been raped, she was, in fact, experiencing FMS created by the suggestion implanted in her mind by that stage hypnotist, who found it funny.

I came across the case of Ann Hazard, in *The Daily Mirror*, who was awarded £20,000 in 1994, after she broke her leg while being a volunteer in a stage hypnosis show, conducted by Robert Halpern. During the show, which took place at the Pavilion Theatre, Glasgow, she asked the hypnotist if she could go to the toilet. He instructed her to take the quickest exit there and back. She then jumped off the stage while in trance and broke her leg.

This may seem a bizarre thing to do under normal circumstances, but while in trance it would seem quite logical. People in a trance react to a suggestion according to what is called "trance logic", which is a literal reaction to a suggestion. During trance the critical intellectualisation of the conscious mind is suspended to a degree, therefore Ann would have been unable to work out that a direct route should have been a safe one. To her, in trance, the direct, quickest route meant just that — the shortest distance between her and the toilet. She had behaved quiet appropriately according to trance logic. If the hypnotist had been properly trained he would have known that this kind of thing could happen, as such knowledge is one of the fundamental principles taught in hypnosis.

The people newspaper in 1994 reported on the stage hypnotist Patrick Charles, also known as Patrick Holden, who, at times, had trouble getting bookings. It is said that on the island of Tenerife one hotel's entertainment manager was so disgusted by his stage act that he refused point blank to book him. It seems most of his show promoted sexual innuendos and crudeness.

According to the article, one woman booked a coach trip to Tenerife's National Park and was unaware of the kind of cavorting that would be going on during the stage hypnosis show that was billed as the entertainment. While in the park she was put into a trance and induced to simulating sex with a blow-up doll. Mother of three Jayne, 29, was reported to have felt truly humiliated by the whole affair. During the act she reached orgasm and cried out in front of a crowd of strangers.

The article went on to say that Jayne did not remember anything that happened after she closed her eyes when she was put into trance, but later she was to see the video, that she reported, was to ruin her life. Many of the people met up in a bar later and to Jayne's horror she saw herself on the screen astride the doll, simulating sex. She became so terrified that people would brand her a slut that she cut off all her hair and dyed it a different colour. She also now lives in the fear that one day her children will see the video and some still photographs that were taken in the park during the show.

Stage hypnotist Alex Le Roy was accused in the *Sun* in 1994 of hypnotising women into believing that he was a fabulous film star and then afterwards leaving some of his subjects wanting to sleep with him. When interviewed, he was reported as saying: "I am a perverted bastard and I live out my sexual fantasies on stage." He further went on to say: "I am an ugly twat and would not have a hope in hell of bedding these women normally."

He said that he has had many complaints, but none legal, usually from boyfriends or spouses, who have gone berserk when he was doing a sex routine with their partner on the stage. Le Roy admitted to hypnotising girls before they sleep with him in order to make them think he is their ultimate sexual fantasy. He said that if they give him permission to hypnotise them then it is the equivalent of giving consent to whatever happens.

He also admitted to having problems with some subjects when things go wrong and has had to call in a hypnotherapist to help remedy the situations.

One of his worst routines described in the article is when he hypnotises a man to believe he is a Father Christmas and a child molester. He hypnotises another to believe he is an eight-year-old boy. I shall not even attempt to describe the kind of scenario that then ensues on stage in the name of entertainment.

In the same newspaper Peter Powers, the stage hypnotist, also bragged that he used hypnosis to get women into bed and that he could get them to do anything he wanted as their sex partners. He billed it as one of the perks of the job. He said in the article that women had the wildest fantasies tucked away in their minds, and he could unlock and enjoy them.

It would be easy here to think that the objections about the use of hypnosis in entertainment centres around the sexual content in many shows, but that would be a false conclusion. Indeed most shows play with sexual innuendo, simulation, and the risqué imagery of having sex with strangers, but for some in the audience that might be all right. However, the majority of people feel profoundly betrayed and vulnerably exposed when this scenario has been unexpectedly played out while they are under the influence of hypnosis. The suspension of the conscious, critical, defensive mechanisms, while in deep somnambulism, leaves some people without the kind of protection against the suggestions offered by these exploitative hypnotists. This can change and ruin their lives.

7

Reviewing the Sharron Tabarn Case

Sharron died on 23rd September 1993 after having taken part as a volunteer in a stage hypnosis show at a pub in Leyland, Lancashire. She was a 24-year-old woman in good health as far as the evidence from her medical records shows.

At the inquest the coroner, Michael Howard McCann (1993) recorded a verdict of death by natural causes, although Sharron's family were not happy with that decision, claiming she was a very healthy young woman who was rarely ill. McCann said that he thought the verdict would be hard for the family to accept.

The death certificate states the cause of death as:

1. Pulmonary Oedema.
2. Inhalation of gastric contents:
Verdict: natural causes.

There was no definite evidence of natural disease, although histological changes in the heart suggested there may have been an underlying defect that produced acute cardiac failure.

Sharron was menstruating at the time. There was no evidence of any drugs having been taken, but alcohol levels of 78mg per 100ml were recorded, which, according to the post-mortem report, is not excessive. It was suggested by the pathologist, Dr Edmund Tapp, that allowing for metabolism this could have stood at over 100mg. Tapp informed the coroner at the inquest that this was the equivalent of three pints of beer. However, subsequently a member of the Central Scientific Laboratories, J P Wootten, suggested that it was possible that Sharron had drunk only three *half* pints of beer. Furthermore, there was no recorded history of any allergic reaction to alcohol. Sharron had never undergone hypnosis before the incident at the show and according to Patricia Andrew, one of the group of three friends who accompanied Sharron that evening, the stage hypnotist had not asked any of the volunteers if they had any phobias.

Tapp found that during the post-mortem a high level of Prolactyn was present in Sharron's body, more than 14 times the normal level. He indicated that this may have meant that she had a fit before she died, although there was no personal history of epilepsy, neurological or heart dysfunction and neither was there any in the family. The current medical knowledge is that Prolactyn is released into the body in reaction to pain.

Because Tapp had not seen any death before that might have been caused in connection with hypnosis, he consulted with Michael Heap, a clinical psychologist who lectures on hypnosis at the University of Sheffield. They concluded that Sharron's death could not be attributed to stage hypnosis.

Heap (1993) made a statement to the police which said, in his opinion, that if anyone has been under any form of stage hypnosis and later becomes ill or distressed, there should be no reason why they should not be able to help themselves or seek help, even if that person had consumed alcohol. He also said that in his opinion there is no connection between hypnosis and adverse side effects.

I believe that Sharron would have made a highly suggestible subject for hypnosis that evening. She had told her girlfriend Pat, even before she arrived at the venue, that she intended to volunteer. Sharron's mother had also seen her before the show and said she was excited about going to see it. Such expectations are considered a constituent part of a good subject for stage hypnosis (McGill 1996).

Sharron had two children by natural childbirth, without the aid of any form of anaesthetic, which, from a psychological point of view, demonstrates a natural ability to disassociate. Kroger (1977), a psychiatrist and anaesthesiollogist acknowledged that women who are able to bear children without chemical anaesthesia have an ability to enter into the trance-like state, either naturally or through training in disassociation techniques.

Further to this Sharron's mother has said that she was a very imaginative and artistic person. The older of two daughters, she had exhibited considerable fantasy oriented play as a child, being satisfied with making up games for herself, and not always seeking new toys, but being quite happy to use the ones she had. She was described as a happy-go-lucky child and known as a very sociable adult who mixed well.

Sheehan (1979) wrote about people who have a good ability to use their imagination and who have trusting temperaments, making very good hypnotic subjects. They can also be very responsive to suggestion when in trance. In short, taking everything into account, Sharron profiles as a stage hypnotist's ideal subject.

In her statement Patricia Andrews says that she attended the stage hypnosis show with Sharron, Sharron's estranged husband Darren, and his friend John. Darren had also gone onto the stage to be hypnotised but had been rejected by the hypnotist as an unsuitable subject.

She goes on to describe how, having stepped up as a volunteer, Sharron was then hypnotised, being taken into a deep somnambulistic state of trance along with the other volunteers. She was put through several tasks, including imitating the pop singer Madonna, seeing the men in the audience with no clothes on (the X-ray specs routine) and kissing a man in the audience. The suggestion given to her to terminate the trance experience was that when the hypnotist said "goodnight" the subjects would feel 10,000 volts of electricity through the seat of their chairs. As the hypnotist did this it seemed to onlookers that she flew off her chair.

When Sharron was 11 years old, according to her parents, she had received an electric shock from a wall switch in the family home and it had thrown her across the room. Her parents reported that from that moment on Sharron had been terrified of electricity and as an adult would not even change a light bulb or a plug. Three or four weeks before her death her father nearly died of an electric shock and was signed off work with burns for five weeks.

With people who suffer phobias the exposure to a specific stimuli brings on an adverse reaction. In hypnosis, when a person is told to imagine that stimuli they react to the imagined stimuli as if it were real (Andreas & Andreas 1989).

After the show Sharron said that she was not feeling well so the group went back to her home. Complaining of a bad headache and dizziness, she went to lie down and slept on the bottom of her youngest daughter's bed, not even bothering to take off any of her clothes. Just after she went to bed, she was adminstered Paracetamol, something which Sharron's mother said was very rare. At 7.00am in the morning her estranged husband Darren, who had stayed over in the same room, heard the children making a noise and when he investigated he found Sharron dead at the bottom of the bed.

In Heap's book *Hypnosis in Therapy* (1991) he talks about early mesmerism not being quite the same as hypnosis, saying that hypnosis today is more the "purposeful induction of a state of trance through verbally conveyed ideas". However, today's hypnotists use all the sensory systems to induce the desired trance-like states (Bandler & Grinder 1981). There are further references to mesmerism inducing a "crisis", something like an epileptic fit.

I agree that the psychodynamics involved in early mesmerism were generally different to modern-day hypnosis (Gauld 1992), but they are much closer than Heap portrays. If mesmerism was not a form of hypnotism, why mention it at all in a book on clinical hypnosis?

Also, if mesmerism came out of exorcism, inducing epileptic-like seizures, why then is it not possible to make stronger associations between Sharron Tabarn's stage hypnosis experience and the fit she may have suffered?

As we have seen earlier, to imply that hypnosis is benign is, in fact, incorrect because its very induction is dependent upon suggestions changing the psychological and physical qualities of the subject. For hypnosis to take place suggestions are required to produce an altered state of awareness, regardless of which communication systems are being used for the induction (visual, auditory, kinaesthetic, olfactory or gustatory). And that altered state will produce bodily changes. Erickson (Rossi (ed) 1989 vol 1) was famous for being able to induce trances using any of those systems.

Furthermore he observed that physiological reactions do take place as a result of suggestions and at times a subject may hallucinate that such physiological reactions are taking place. While in hypnosis, developing the belief that something is happening can be as real to the person's subjective perceptions, as if that experience was really happening (Rossi (ed) 1989 vol 1).

Therefore hypnosis equals the consequences of suggestions and a change in physiological as well as psychological processes, causing the trance-like state. Not all inductions or trance-like states, however, are the same and not all produce a lessening of heart rate, lowering of blood pressure or a soporific state.

If we consider the bodily changes that take place in profound states of trance, where activities can be energetic as well as soporific, then motivation induced through suggestion means that the hypnotic process can never be benign. This begs the question of how wide the definition of hypnosis can be spread. I choose the expansionist model to spread the definition of hypnosis to all states of altered consciousness induced through suggestion.

I realise that a dilemma arises when including waking trance. For some clinicians, this may be classified along the lines of the social compliance theory (Spanos 1996) and negates hypnosis being classified as a special altered state of awareness. However, this brings us to the point of view of Wolinsky (1991) that people are permanently in trances, and that they simply move from one trance to another, with hypnosis being the influence by which suggestion alters the trance.

For Sharron Tabarn then she may have gone home in a different trance state from the one in which she arrived at the venue that evening. The new trance may have contained the post-hypnotic dangers of a massive abreaction to the suggestion that when she woke up she would feel 10,000 volts of electricity going through her body.

I suggest that Sharron never woke up from the trance on the stage, but went home, fell asleep and then woke up reacting to the above post-hypnotic suggestion. This, compounded with her phobia of electricity, caused an epileptic-like seizure and in sheer terror she had a heart attack, vomited and choked to death on the contents of her stomach.

Is pain registered at some unconscious level but ignored by the conscious mind?

If we consider the work of the respected researchers from Stanford University, the Hilgards (1994), who have studied hidden pain extensively, we can look at Sharron's possible hidden pain.

According to the Hilgards pain, and suffering derived from pain seem to be a neurological indicator of physical, mental, emotional, social, and even spiritual disturbance of the organism's homeostasis. The registration of the pain sensory experiences fluctuates from unconscious to conscious awareness eg hunger, blisters, toothache, psychological distress.

Since the unconscious mind runs the involuntary functions, it is logical to assume that all disturbance is registered at an unconscious level, but not necessarily at a conscious level. Pain reaches a threshold level, forcing it into conscious awareness, requiring the person to have extra focuses of attention, in order to change the circumstances and alleviate the pain.

Overt pain is the open behavioural display of both conscious and unconscious awareness of discomfort from noxious external stimuli, internal disturbance or a hallucinated experience of either of the previous.

Covert pain is the unconscious registration of pain, without it being brought to conscious attention, ignored by consciousness or through the unconscious processes purposefully keeping it from consciousness.

Experimentally it is possible to demonstrate the existence of hidden or covert pain that is kept from consciousness (Hilgard & Hilgard 1994). During hypnosis a hypnotist can tell a subject to consciously ignore the pain and they can do that. By monitoring the heart beat, hormone levels and muscle tonality during this process it can be observed that the subject is displaying the physiological signs of the pain experience, without being consciously aware.

Therefore pain can be registered at an unconscious level without the conscious mind being aware of the distress, hidden for whatever reason the unconscious mind has for keeping it solely in a particular part of the unconscious.

Jung spoke of the differing egos that came to and from consciousness, according to their need to function at the executive level. Virginia Satir (1988), the American therapist, talked of our psyche being composed of many different parts, and some of her work on internal conflict consists of getting one part to talk to another. The American hypnotist Hammond (1995) referred to the Control Room Technique, where the therapist talks to the relevant control mechanism within the subject's psyche. Erickson (Rossi (ed) 1989 vol 3) reported experiments with automatic writing, where he communicated with separate personality aspects, in different sensory systems, at the same time.

This splitting of consciousness into many factions, far from being a pathology, is now considered a natural part of normal psychological processing. We have a part for running our heart, changing our blood, checking our state of happiness, and even doing the shopping. In fact we have parts for doing everything in our experiential existence.

One of those parts is a defence mechanism that sometimes wakes someone up out of hypnosis if a suggestion is made that is contrary to their well-being. However, I believe that in hypnosis this part does not work every time in some people. Suggestions can be made during hypnosis that are contrary to the subject's well-being, but sometimes, due to organic or existing cognitive processes, that defensive part fails to activate.

If we look at people who have been subjected to an abusive childhood and who later turn up for therapy, it is plain to see that suggestions which were made to them can have the effect of producing a negative self-image; even though those suggestions will have been contrary to that person's well-being, they may have been accepted and incorporated into the personality (Bass & Davis 1988).

With many men who suffer from impotency, I have observed that it can often be the result of a single comment made to them that has instantly suppressed their sexual ego prowess. The same may be said of many human behaviours that have resulted from even the smallest of innuendoes. So when we enter into the hypnotic equation I propose that a subject can, indeed, be severely damaged by a hypnotist's careless suggestions, and accept what would normally be considered a harmful suggestion.

I know that some theorists reading this will now be able to bring out a set of papers written on suggestions made that are contrary to a subject's well-being. These papers will show experiments where the subjects have overridden suggestions to steal or maim another person. However, such experiments are not a process of observation and can be corrupted by their very own design, since they are artificially constructed circumstances.

Erickson carried out such experiments (Rossi (ed) 1989 vol 1), where the subject rejected suggestions contradictory to their normal moral code. He commented afterwards that there is the possibility that his results were part of the constructs of the experimental situation. The subjects, at a deep unconscious level, would know that it was an experiment and a part of their minds would still obey social rules in order to please the experimenter.

So, taking all these considerations into account in the

Sharron Tabarn case, I propose that several things could have happened to her that evening:

1. She was capable of being a very good hypnotic subject and was also a very suggestible person.

2. She was very responsive to the hypnotist's suggestions and performed according to his instructions.

3. There was a profound expectation present in her that what the hypnotist suggested, she believed would come true.

4. There had been no warning that the absolute trust she had probably placed in the hypnotist was going to be betrayed by the suggestion of one of her worst fears: an electric shock.

5. When that happened a part of her reacted to the post-hypnotic suggestion, a defensive part protected her from it and another part suspended the full reaction from taking place at that time. She experienced covert pain, but little overt pain.

6. The waking suggestion of feeling 10,000 volts of electricity did not, in fact, bring her out of trance — she remained somnabulistic. Instead it acted as a time delayed post-hypnotic or even intrahypnotic (a suggestion-reaction that takes place within the hypnotic context) suggestion.

7. At some unconscious level this suggestion waited to be activated to its fullest potential until she woke up.

8. Having gone to sleep she dreamed and her unconscious processed that concealed post-hypnotic/intrahypnotic suggestion, which activated as she slept or began to wake.

9. Experiencing the full terror of an abreaction that the suggestion produced, she had an epileptic fit, which induced a heart attack, causing her to vomit and she was unable to seek help before she choked to death.

If hypnosis is some kind of behavioural regression back to infantile processing of information (Fromm 1979) then there is the possibility that Sharron could have suffered night terrors (Chokroverty, MD, 1994) in deep sleep, which are common to children. Let us also remember that she never made it to her own bed that night, but curiously went to sleep at the bottom of her daughter's single bed, something her family said she had never done before.

Chokroverty (1994) tells us that Hippocrates described fears, rages, delirium and leaps out of bed that occur during sleep. Aristotle observed that many cases of epilepsy started in bed. We also know that some people describe a sense of being locked into the stage hypnosis process, unable to regain control over their situations.

Alcohol can increase the chances of an epileptic fit, but we must remember that Sharron had not consumed a great amount and it had never had an adverse effect on her before. Not only can epilepsy turn into sleep, but sleep can also turn into epilepsy (Chokroverty, MD, 1994).

It is common for subjects in states of trance to have an abreaction when faced with their worst fears or memories. For this reason the majority of hypnotherapists do not practice abreactive work, knowing that it can have unpredictable changes on the subjects' psychology and physiology. One of the problems with taking the subject into a traumatic mind set, is that it can cause considerable dysfunction, from which the subject can suffer renewed posttraumatic stress.

Woolger (1987) wrote about people, who, during pastlife regression, believed they remembered being choked to death, burned alive or suffered other physical injury. In trance these subjects literally do sometimes manifest physiological signs of incurring those injuries.

Raginsky (Kroger 1977) revivified a state of cardiac arrest in a patient by post-hypnotic suggestion to relive an earlier heart attack. And stigmata is the perfect example of where the individual believes they are suffering the crucifixion of Christ and holes do actually appear in their bodies (Early & Lifschutz, 1974, Kroger 1977).

The argument against my considerations of Sharron Tabarn's death is that much of what I propose may be termed to be pure superstition. However, I base my conclusions on deductive reasoning. A young healthy woman, who experienced no major illnesses, dies five hours after a stage hypnosis show, where she received the kind of suggestion that could be perceived as being life threatening. The pathologist can find no explicable cause of death, other than the kind of symptoms that may be common to someone who has died as the result of a hypnotic abreaction.

To be fair to all involved, absolute, conclusive evidence may never have been offered the coroner in this case. Having considered the facts in this case I personally am in no doubt that Sharron Tabarn would have more than likely been alive the next morning had she not undergone stage hypnosis.

Heap said in his paper, *A Case of Death Following Stage Hypnosis: Analysis and Implications*, University of Sheffield, that he found it hard to consider Sharron's death to be a result of post-hypnotic suggestion with any seriousness. In his explanation of this he attempted to claim that all changes associated with hypnosis are derived from psychological, subjective experience and physiological changes tended to be comparatively unexceptional or even absent altogether. But what about the placebo effect?

He talks about the hypnotic subject's experience being an "as if" frame where the individual is not really having physiological changes but is only imagining that they are. However, if this were so, why practice hypnosis with medicine at all?

Heap tries to comment that the effects of hypnosis are not dramatic, but how can he judge other people's subjective experiences? Of course he can quote chapter and verse to support his argument; however, I become astounded when he writes on the subjective interpretation of 10,000 volts of electricity. He says that "the circumstances of stage hypnosis call for a benign and humorous interpretation of an electric shock rather than one which entails the realistic enactment of a traumatic and fatal incident". How could he possibly know what Sharron's subjective interpretation of that suggestion was?

Heap's partial redemption is that in his analysis he said

he could not prove that the stage hypnosis was *not* responsible for Sharron's death and that it was not a comfortable feeling for him to know this.

He also says that the ingredients in stage hypnosis have, in recent history, been over exploited by some entertainers, and participants may be coerced into behaving in a shameful and degrading manner in front of the audience. Along with that he comments that we should not be surprised if these people feel confused, distressed and humiliated when they try to make sense of their behaviour after the event.

Dr Prem Misra, a consultant psychiatrist and chairperson of the academic committee of the British Society of Medical and Dental hypnosis, wrote to Margaret Harper, Sharron's mother. The letter said that he was sorry to hear about her daughter's death and explained that the society had long campaigned for the banning of stage hypnosis.

When Heap wrote an article called *The Nature of Hypnosis* in *The Psychologist* (November 1996) there was some disagreement with his views. A letter to the journal in February 1997 criticised the article and suggested the author largely ignored other explanations of hypnosis.

Now let us consider the possibility of death by belief, which is not uncommon. There have been many recorded cases of death through inexplicable causes with people who have died believing they have a Voodoo curse upon them (Rigaud 1985). Many of the early explorers into Africa noted and documented such cases.

In other cultures there are rituals that are based around a person wishing themselves to death, believing that their life has come to the end of its usefulness.

In Haitian culture priests do convince some people, with the aid of poisons and expansionist hypnosis, that they are zombies and have been brought back from the dead (*The Serpent and the Rainbow*, Universal, 1987; *To the Ends of the Earth: Interview with a Zombie*, Channel Four, 1997). In fact many of these priests have been tried and convicted for this perceived sorcery.

Among the half-castes of Guatemala magical procedures can kill. *Susto or Aspanto* occurs when victims fall stone dead and are later revived by ritualistic ceremonies of the magician (Kroger 1977).

Stanislav Grof (1988), the former chief of psychiatric research at Maryland Psychiatric Research Centre, discusses in his book *The Adventure of Self-discovery*, the human ability to psychologically alter the body via thought, a concept which is now accepted by Western science. For thousands of years the yogis have practised extraordinary physiological feats of changing their heart rates, slowing and reducing their capacity of breathing, varying body temperature and surviving without food or water for long periods.

One case I experienced personally was with the parents of a close friend of mine. In the mid 1970s his father developed cancer and was simply lying in bed waiting to die. His mother, who was devoted to her husband, tended to his father's every need at the bedside. One afternoon his father died at 5.00pm. Then his mother went over to the dressing table, brushed her hair, laid down next to her husband's body and also died. At his mother's inquest no cause of death could be found.

Another friend of mine from a Native American culture told me about the tradition in her tribe. Many years ago, before the white man arrived, if a husband died the old wife would go out into the snow and just sit there and wait to die. Life for them was hard and the old women believed they had outgrown their usefulness and would be a burden to their relatives.

These examples may not be the same as the post-hypnotic trauma that Sharron Tabarn may have suffered, but they do demonstrate the principle of death by belief, which is undeniably a reality.

Our belief systems are part of the drivers of our behaviours that not only influence our psychology, but also help create aspects of our physiology (Dilts, Hallbom & Smith 1990). It is commonly accepted that the psychological mind sets that exist bear upon a patient's condition, and can determine who will recover well from an illness and

141

who will not.

In cases of cancer hypnosis is now used to improve the prognosis and change the physiology of the patient (Simonton, Matthews-Simonton & Creighton 1978). In Texas the Simontons have documented many cases, some terminally ill, who have changed their life-threatening diagnosis, using techniques of hypnotic, creative visualisation.

Ernest Rossi PhD, (1993), a psychologist and hypnotherapist, has published work on changes to the body's immune system and chemistry through the power of hypnosis and mind control techniques. Far from being just theory based suppositions, he has shown that microbiological examination of tissue and blood samples shows a marked difference, in controlled studies, after a person was hypnotised and healing suggestions were made to them.

Hirshberg & Barasch (1995) profiled many cases of people who change their physical destinies due to their belief of whether they would live or die after their diagnosed illnesses.

Undoubtedly psychology changes physiology and I disagree when Heap says that these effects are simply psychological perceptions. His is an attempt to validate psychology as the only real viewpoint. The evidence I have shown suggests that neither hypnosis nor the suggestions delivered by hypnosis can be completely benign. Whether at an organ functionality or molecular level there is sufficient evidence to prove, beyond reasonable doubt, that hypnosis has a profound effect on the human condition.

People do die of fright, throughout different cultures, even though it can be an unexplainable pathology when trying to determine the cause of death during an autopsy. "Died of fright" is not something that a pathologist wants to put on a death certificate because it may be perceived as being unscientific and indecisive. In my opinion, "died of natural causes" was the incorrect deductive reason to put on Sharron Tabarn's death certificate because, through a process of logical deduction, the hypnosis was the extraordinary fact that preceded death.

Heap asks in his paper why there is an urge by both

professionals and lay people to convict the stage hypnotist "on the basis of the most indeterminate set of ideas and evidence". But what of Sharron Tabarn's family?

The loss they have suffered by her premature death has been devastating to them. Two small children were left without a mother. The father of those children was left with the burden of bringing them up as a single parent. Her parents and sister also suffered a great loss and continue to feel cheated.

The family feel they need what they believe is the real cause of her death to be recognised so they can complete their grieving process. Sharron's mother believes this process is not able to come to its full conclusion because of the verdict of death by natural causes.

There is also the consideration of compensation for the hardships her family and children have and will suffer from Sharron not being around, and for their sense of loss. Why should stage hypnosis be exempt of blame?

At the time of writing this book the attorney general has just granted permission to Sharron's mother to seek to reopen the case. The family hope that stage hypnosis will eventually be banned as a form of entertainment, as it is in many other countries

8

The View Of The Experts

"As with any treatment do no harm to the patient"

Hippocrates

Literature references

The British Medical Journal published a paper on the *Medical Use of Hypnotism* in 1955. It recognised the therapeutic applications and uses of hypnotism, expressing a continuing strong disapproval of public exhibitions of hypnotic phenomena and hoped that some legal restriction would be placed on them.

In the 1950s the American Medical Association also took the same stance as the British, but again their voice was ineffective and their government ignored the advice and recommendations given to prohibit hypnosis in entertainment.

Erickson recorded having encountered more than a score of patients who had suffered strange back problems (Rossi 1989 vol 1). The common denominator between all of the subjects was that they had been volunteers in stage hypnosis shows.

Each had demonstrated the human plank trick when experiencing catalepsy and body rigidity. The volunteer was then suspended horizontally between two chairs by the head and feet. Sometimes people sat or walked on the suspended volunteer. Erickson said that this unnatural act, known as the "human bridge" could well have been the source of these patients' back problems.

Kroger MD (1977), who practised and taught hypnosis over four decades, talks of how few casualities there are that come to light. He states that he is opposed to entertainment hypnotists using hypnosis in any manner. He believes that, irrespective of their technical ability in inducing hypnosis, the stage hypnotist does not know the emotional make-up of the person they are hypnotising. Without that knowledge, he says, they are inviting trouble for themselves and the subject.

He comments that because stage hypnosis is not a therapeutic relationship, the subject has no symptoms to lose that may be servicing a need (secondary gain), therefore they may be more predisposed to suggestibility. There is also the implication that because stage hypnosis involves the expectation of entertainment, ridiculous suggestions may be more readily accepted.

In 1978 Dr David Waxman wrote to the *British Medical Journal* emphasising a warning against unqualified individuals practising hypnosis; included in this category were stage hypnotists.

Bandler and Grinder (1981) spoke of how the word "hypnosis" elicited strong reactions from people. They noted how some of the public view hypnosis as only good for making others behave like chickens on the stage or for a hoax. This statement, as logical as it may seem, is noteworthy when we consider that Bandler set up a British training course for his form of hypnosis in 1996 with Paul McKenna, a man who is an ongoing stage hypnotist.

Clinical Hypnosis: Principles and Applications: Second Edition (1985) by Crasilneck PhD & Hall MD has in the preface the following statement: "Our own judgment remains clear: hypnotic techniques should be used only by well-trained and licensed professionals who are capable of treating the same problems without the use of hypnosis."

Scottish consultant psychiatrist Dr Prem Misra talked about the problem with shows in his part of the world at the 1985 International Congress on Hypnosis and Psychosomatic Medicine, in Toronto. One case involved an addiction to Spanish onions that came about after a stage hypnotist had made the suggestion that they were tasty to the subject during a show. Another case dealt with a person who had a compulsion to do a striptease when someone clapped their hands. He talked about nausea, tiredness, fits, blackouts, depression, anxiety and exacerbating of mental illness suffered by people who had been hypnotised during a stage show.

He mentioned one subject who became addicted to appearing on stage and actually went to be hypnotised more than 300 times, in the end becoming suicidal. Dr Misra has asked the Scottish Office to curb the activities of stage hypnosis shows after the disturbing rise in the number of patients suffering from side effects.

MacHovec (1986), an American clinical psychologist, recorded the most profound collection of cases in his book *Hypnosis Complications*. He opens with the case of a young woman who went into a life-threatening catatonic seizure shortly after being involved in a stage hypnosis show and was hospitalised for a week, reported by Kleinhauz and Beran (1981, p 148-161). He cites cases from ancient Egypt, through to Freud and modern-day clinical journals, many of which report complications that can occur with hypnosis.

He says that these often unpredictable symptoms can range from severe life-threatening emergencies, personality changes or psychotic episodes, to mild, transient, unpleasant thoughts and feelings that fade within minutes. Frequently reported side effects, he says, are headaches, anxiety, irritability, fatigue, depression, unexplained weeping, dizziness, disturbed sleep or dreams, fear or panic attacks, lowered stress threshold, poor coping skills, depersonalisation, derealisation, disorientation, obsessive rumination, delusions, psychomotor retardation, impaired or distorted memory, Attention Deficit Disorder, psychotic decompression, concentration difficulties, sexual problems, antisocial behaviour, symptom exaggeration, Post-Traumatic Stress Disorder, and, at the extreme, death.

He discusses how more stage entertainers are involved in reports of complications with greater severity than in the clinical or experimental setting. There was a girl who developed 150 spontaneous trances in 30 days after being hypnotised on stage. Two other girls were reported to have experienced spontaneous trances after the show and one collapsed. There was a case of hospitalisation and the need for six months of orthopaedic and psychiatric treatment for a woman who had performed the human plank trick. Another case was a young man who developed a compulsion for onions for five years after being a volunteer in a show.

MacHovec also discusses how some subjects awoke when they had obnoxious suggestions made to them, but some did not, instead accepting the suggestion and complying with it. His opinion is that conducting hypnosis without training and supervision is dangerous and can result in severe complications and side effects. There is also the consideration that with such large audiences as stage hypnosis draws, it is impossible to pay sufficient attention to the committee because the entertainment demands are too great.

As well as discussing the possibility of complications occurring in the clinical and experimental situation, he suggests that as many as one in twenty people taking part in stage hypnosis may suffer adverse reactions.

MacHovec's publication should really be statutory reading for all trainers and trainees in hypnosis, but the reality is that so few courses spend any time at all paying attention to what damage can be done by the misuses of hypnosis. Generally hypnosis trainers prefer to gloss over this possibility and concentrate on presenting hypnosis as the mystical, inexplicable cure-all. By presenting their trainings in this way many schools tend to believe that they are offering students the dream of going out and curing the world, and the selling of such abilities is, of course, extremely profitable. Unfortunately the truth is that there are thousands of hypnotists who simply have little idea of what they are doing, but they believe they are the next saviour. In fact they are doing an incredible amount of harm to naive and unsuspecting subjects.

Echterling & Emmerling published a paper in the *American Journal of Clinical Hypnosis* in 1987 entitled *Impact of Stage*

Hypnosis. It assessed the impact of a stage hypnosis performance on a university campus. The study determined that the performance had both positive and negative effects upon a number of the participants. It further went on to say that stage hypnosis poses risks that are unacceptable and outweighed its potential entertainment value and therapeutic benefits.

John Hartland (Waxman (ed) 1989) talks about how he considers that stage hypnosis abuses, devalues and degrades the subjects. He further goes on to warn about classical cases reported on a variety of consequences suffered by volunteers, ranging from panic reactions, schizophrenia, psychosis and suicide.

Scheflin & Shapiro (1989) consider the legal aspects of hypnosis, a consensus of clinical opinions and the way in which the law may be applied to hypnosis. They identify three groups of professionals that are regularly engaged in the practice of hypnosis: medical, dental and health professionals; lay hypnotists (not including stage performers); law enforcement personnel.

Gauld (1992) documents countless recorded historical opinions that disagree with hypnosis being used for entertainment. There are references to it being banned in different places over a period of 200 years. While such bans were often made at times by religious institutions for fear of diabolic practices, the majority are by the medical profession who had identified potential risks of damage to subjects.

A paper appeared in the *Australian Journal of Clinical Hypnosis* in 1994 by Robb O Stanley, the president of the Australian Society of Clinical Hypnosis, which looked at the protection of the uses of hypnosis. His findings concluded that side effects did occur at times with hypnosis, both in clinical and other settings and ranged from mild disturbances to the occurrence of psychotic episodes.

When I spoke to him he told me that although they have some regulations in Australia against the public performance of hypnosis for entertainment, it is not the case in all the states. He was also resigned to the fact that these regulations were not being upheld because the police simply did not understand them or could see no harm in what was happening.

He went on to say that hypnosis in the entertainment context is fraught with many risks and the lack of adequate screening, follow-up and the debriefing is a major concern. The failure to de-hypnotise highly suggestible members of the audience, together with inadequate suggestion removal, poses significant risks. He concludes that on this basis, and for the image of therapeutic hypnosis, its practice in relation to entertainment ought not to be sanctioned.

In response to the case of Ann Hazard who was awarded £20,000 after breaking her leg during a stage hypnosis show in 1994, having being misdirected by the stage hypnotist Robert Halpern, the following comment was made in the *Daily Mail* by Dr Myer Seltzer, past president of the British Society of Medical and Dental Hypnosis: "We are one of the few countries in the world that does not have regulations and the dangers are horrendous."

In the *British Journal of Psychiatry* in 1995 a psychiatrist called D S Allen described a case of schizophrenia induced by stage hypnosis.

In *Hypnotic Induction and Suggestion*, the publication of the American Society of Clinical Hypnosis (1995), edited by D Corydon Hammond, PhD, the ex-president, there is a section on stage hypnosis and complications of hypnosis. It advises against stage hypnosis performances, commenting that many of the complications reported are the result of the use of hypnosis for entertainment.

In 1995 the National Register of Hypnotherapists conducted *A Survey of Personal Stage Experiences* in England. In the conclusion it said that it is a most indisputable fact, revealed by the survey, that there can be longlasting or serious side effects from stage hypnosis. It commented that because of these consequences it had no place as a form of entertainment. A copy of this survey was sent to the Home Office prior to the 1996 review on stage hypnosis.

Crussell (1996) profiled several cases in the *European Journal of Clinical Hypnosis,* of people who had suffered physical, mental and emotional damage after having been volunteers in stage hypnosis shows. His patients include cases of broken limbs, headaches, dizziness, and in the severest of cases hypnotically induced schizophrenia.

It is clear from present literature that the process of stage hypnosis for entertainment purposes, although it appears to be nothing more than harmless fun to the untrained eye, can be a dangerous, harmful and damaging process.

Professional associations and training institutions
The world is a very diverse place with many varying perspectives, not only in different cultures but also with each society, sect, cult, discipline or school of thought.

Israel is very suspicious in the way it views hypnosis and has laws preventing it, which is strange because the early Jews practised hypnosis. In Switzerland, Sweden, Norway, Denmark, Holland, Belgium, Germany, and France entertainment hypnosis is illegal. Among the states of America that do not permit it are Oregon, Montana, South Dakota, Nebraska, Kansas, Tennessee, and all the US military bases. The Canadian province of Ontario also does not permit stage hypnosis.

Therefore within this section no definitive, concrete opinion on the use of hypnosis for entertainment purposes and its attributes or consequences can be offered. What I present is a diverse collection of opinions, beliefs and attitudes.

CATEGORY A

ESTABLISHMENTS WITH PROHIBITIONS
The following are professional societies, institutions, association and schools, which strictly prohibit their members or students from participating in or conducting stage hypnosis for entertainment purposes. Should members or students partake in this activity they may be subject to

disciplinary action.
American Medical Association (Association of MDs)
They have gone on record as saying that while they recognise the use of hypnosis as a genuine and valid therapeutic tool, they condemn the use of hypnosis for entertainment purposes.
American Society of Clinical Hypnosis (Association)
All members are prohibited from partaking in stage hypnosis and the association wishes for it to be made illegal.
The Atkinson Ball College of Hypnotherapy & Hypnohealing (College)
All students are prohibited from partaking in stage hypnosis.
Australian Medical Association (Association of MDs)
In a reply to my enquiry they stated that any practitioner who practised stage hypnosis would be in breach of their code of ethics. Their directive to their members is to treat people with compassion and they do not believe stage hypnosis does this. Any member partaking in such an activity would be subject to disciplinary review.
Australian Society of Hypnosis (Association)
All members are prohibited from partaking in stage hypnosis and the association wishes for it to be made illegal. When I contacted Dr Robb O Stanley, a past president, he said there had been dreadful problems with stage hypnosis over the years. I further learnt that a stage hypnotist had tried to sue him for speaking out in public against it.

I also interviewed Dr Wendy-Louise Walker, another past president, who said she had encountered cases of subjects who had suffered badly after being involved in stage hypnosis. She was also outraged that the controls on the use of hypnosis were actually being slackened during 1997 and not tightened up as she and the association would have wished. She believes that the ridicule that takes place during these shows is just too much for some personalities to withstand.
British Hypnosis Research (School and Association)
All members and students are prohibited from partaking in stage hypnosis. Stephen Brooks, the president, has said it should be banned.

British Hypnotherapy Association (Association)

All members are prohibited from partaking in stage hypnosis and the association wishes for it to be made illegal.

British Institute of Hypnotherapy (Association)

All members are prohibited from partaking in stage hypnosis and the association wishes for it to be made illegal.

British Medical Association (Association of MDs)

The BMA appointed a psychological subcommittee to consider the use of hypnotism. It recognised the many uses of hypnosis as a tool in the assistance of achieving therapeutic goals. It issued a warning that if misused, without proper consideration, hypnosis could have dangerous effects upon subjects. The subcommittee's report expressed strong disapproval for using hypnosis for public exhibitions of entertainment.

British Medical Hypnotherapy Examinations Board

The governing body of this board are of the opinion that hetero-hypnosis should not be used by untrained or unqualified individuals. They also believe that the use of hypnosis in entertainment is upredictable and dangerous.

British Register of Complementary Practitioners (Institute of Complementary Medicine) (Association)

All members are prohibited from partaking in stage hypnosis.

British Society of Clinical Hypnotherapists (Association)

All members are prohibited from partaking in stage hypnosis and the association wishes for it to be made illegal.

British Society of Experimental and Clinical Hypnosis (Association)

All members are prohibited from partaking in stage hypnosis. Some of their members wish for stricter licensing laws rather than a complete ban.

British Society of Medical & Dental Hypnosis (Association)

All members are prohibited from partaking in stage hypnosis and the association wishes for it to be made illegal.

Canadian Hypnosis Association (Association)

All members are prohibited from partaking in stage hypnosis.

Central Association of Psychotherapists (Association)
All members are prohibited from partaking in stage hypnosis.

Central Register of Advanced Hypnotherapists (Association)
All members are prohibited from partaking in stage hypnosis.

Centre Training School of Hypnotherapy & Psychotherapy (School)
All students are prohibited from partaking in stage hypnosis.

Corporation of Advanced Hypnotherapy (Association)
All members are prohibited from partaking in stage hypnosis.

The Institute of Clinical Hypnosis (School)
All students are prohibited from partaking in stage hypnosis.

International Society of Hypnosis (Association)
All members are prohibited from partaking in stage hypnosis and the association wishes for it to be made illegal.

Irish Institute of Counselling & Hypnotherapy (School)
All students are prohibited from partaking in stage hypnosis.

London College of Clinical Hypnosis (School)
All students are prohibited from partaking in stage hypnosis and the school wishes for it to made illegal.

National College of Hypnosis & Psychotherapy (School)
All students are prohibited from partaking in stage hypnosis and the association wishes for it to be made illegal.

National Register of Hypnotherapists and Psychotherapists (Association)
All members are prohibited from partaking in stage hypnosis and the association wishes for it to be made illegal.

National School of Hypnosis & Advanced Psychotherapy (School)
All students are prohibited from partaking in stage hypnosis.

New Zealand Society of Hypnosis (Association)
All members are prohibited from partaking in stage hyp-

nosis and the association wishes for it to be made illegal.

Psychotherapy & Hypnosis Training Association (Association)

All members are prohibited from partaking in stage hypnosis.

Royal College of Psychiatrists (Association)

Members of this body are governed by the code of ethics of the General Medical Council. The British, American and Australian medical bodies have clearly expressed their strong opposition to the use of hypnosis in any form of entertainment.

South African Association of Clinical Hypnosis (Association)

All members are prohibited from partaking in stage hypnosis.

United Kingdom Council of Psychotherapists (Association)

All members are prohibited from partaking in stage hypnosis.

University of London

All students are prohibited from partaking in stage hypnosis.

University of Sheffield

All students are bound by an Ethical Code based on the Ethical Guidelines of the British Society of Experimental and Clinical Hypnosis, which forbids them from using hypnosis for entertainment purposes. However, the tutor Michael Heap pointed out in a letter to me that "this aspect of the Ethical Code is probably not one which is enforceable by the threat of any disciplinary action. That is, it would probably be illegal for the course examiners to penalise students or prevent them gaining their qualification because of their engaging in the above activity". So, it would seem that the students here are bound by an unenforceable code.

When I started to canvas and log the professionals who were not only prohibited from partaking in stage hypnosis, but also believed it should be made illegal, I got as far as the million mark, went into a trance and decided that you could figure it out for yourselves.

CATEGORY B

ESTABLISHMENTS WITHOUT PROHIBITIONS

The following are some of the establishments that did not have clauses in their codes of ethics or articles of memorandum which prohibited members or students from partaking in stage hypnosis for entertainment purposes.

"The hottest corners of hell are reserved for those who, in a moment of crisis, maintained their neutrality"

Chicken Soup for The Soul Vol II

American Institute of Hypnotherapy (College)

This is the institute at which I am currently taking my doctorate in Clinical Hypnotherapy during the writing of this book. The AIH is recognised by and registered with the California Board of Education. Although I have found the standard very high, I am in the embarrassing position of having to inform the reader that this school teaches stage hypnosis, much to my disapproval. To be true to my research I have had no other choice but to mention this.

It is only one of their very numerous courses, the others of which I have the greatest respect for. It is my earnest hope that they will, in the future, be able to move on from their present position.

Despite my having presented a paper to them on the dangers of stage hypnosis, cataloguing classic literature supporting the need to stop this practice, my protestations have been ignored. I was unaware that this was their position when I enrolled with them, but I am continuing with my doctorate.

American Board of Hypnotherapy (Association)

I resigned from this association due to their refusal to implement guidelines to members preventing the involvement of therapists in stage hypnosis. After presenting several communications to this organisation, they would not budge and refused to include an exclusion clause in their code of ethics.

Association of Neuro Linguistic Programmers (England) (Association)

I remember Richard Bandler, one of the founders of NLP, saying at a presentation in Kensington in 1995 to over a thousand people: "When they did not let me practise hypnosis I called it NLP." In fact Bandler is to be no less than congratulated for bringing hypnosis into more popular use through his approaches.

The funny thing is when I wrote to the ANLP I got a letter back saying they only practised psychotherapy and counselling, and those members wishing to include hypnosis or hypnotherapy would need to take further training. I think this is what NLP practitioners would identify as incongruent.

NLP is undoubtedly composed, for a large part, of hypnotic techniques, and there are no clauses in ANLP's codes of ethics to protect the public from practitioners using hypnosis for entertainment. For this reason, I did not renew my membership.

The British Psychological Society (Association)

I also resigned from this society due to their refusal to implement guidelines to members concerning the involvement of therapists in stage hypnosis.

Again I presented material to this organisation, as many of its practitioners use hypnosis, but I could not convince the BPS to include a prohibition clause in their code of ethics.

I should also point out that the president of the BPS, Chris Cullen, sat on the panel for the 1996 government review of stage hypnosis. The panel's views are not shared by many of the members of the BPS and Dr Richard Woolfson wrote the following in the November 1996 edition of *The Psychologist:*

"Stage shows have done to hypnosis what BSE has done to British beef. Not suprisingly the sight of a member of the audience being hypnotised and made to perform a ridiculous and humiliating behavioural routine for the sole purpose of making others laugh tends to reduce our belief in the value of hypnosis as anything other than a tool for generating fun."

In the June 1997 edition of *The Psychologist*, Cullen said in an interview that society policy should be formed by the members, from the bottom up rather than in a top down fashion. These ideas, although being noble, do not seem to transpire into reality. There are many members of this society who possess a wealth of experience in hypnosis, and in my opinion, at least one of them should have been offered a seat on the review panel.

The James Braid Society (Association)

James Braid was the doctor from the north of England, who coined the phrase "hypnosis" back in the 19th century. He was a medical man and a member of the British medical association of that time, which strongly disapproved of hypnosis being used in entertainment. This society was formed in London as a club for those involved in the ethical practice of hypnosis, in order that they may transcend schools and associations and meet on a casual and social basis.

At its inaugural meeting in March 1997 part of the proposed draft constitution was to prohibit those involved in any way with stage hypnosis from being members. However, several people turned up to that meeting who wanted stage hypnotists to be let in. Consequently a second inaugural meeting was held in November 1997, but many of the original members did not attend. The American ex-stage hypnotist Gill Boyne, who was not a member, turned up and took the floor and the vote was passed to allow stage hypnotists in.

This subsequently caused an enormous uproar among the members, many of whom said they would not continue to be a part of the society if that ruling stood. At the time of press the battle continues and the decision may yet be overturned.

National Council of Hypnotherapists (Association)

I also resigned from this association due to their refusal to implement guidelines to members concerning the involvement of therapists in stage hypnosis, thereby, in my opinion, failing to protect the public interest. Although they stated that they disapproved of stage hypnosis they would not infringe on the personal liberty of any member wishing to participate in the activity.

National Council of Psychotherapists (Association)

My fourth resignation was from this association due to their refusal to implement guidelines to members concerning the involvement of therapists in stage hypnosis.

The NCH & NCP were linked organisations that shared a common quarterly magazine. In order to get the membership to put a clause in their code of ethics I wrote a brief article and sent it to the magazine. The article was sent back with a letter telling me there was no room in the magazine. This letter was from the editor, Dylan Morgan, who had included in the previous journal 13 pages of exerpts from a chapter of one of his unpublished books. The piece was entitled *The Defensive Persona*. There are presently no prohibitions stopping members working as both stage hypnotists as well as hypnotherapists.

Perhaps the majority of the members may be happy with a clause in the code of ethics prohibiting members from partaking in stage hypnosis, but my opinions were not allowed to be presented to them.

The United Kingdom Central Council for Nursing, Midwifery and Health Visiting (Association)

Although they produce several booklets on professional conduct and guidelines, there is no specific clause preventing its members from partaking in stage hypnosis.

CATEGORY C

ESTABLISHMENTS WHICH DID NOT WISH TO REPLY

The following establishments cannot go in either of the above categories, as I cannot say whether they have prohibitions or not, as they did not wish to say.

United Kingdom College of Complementary Health Care Studies (College)

When I wrote to this college I did not get a reply, so I telephoned and spoke to Mandy Langford, one of the proprietors, to clarify the situation. I was told that they would not be giving a written response and that what her students did after they left her college was not under her control. The stage hypnotist Paul McKenna has given lectures here.

The British Government Review of Stage Hypnosis

On the 12th December 1994 an adjournment debate was held at the House of Commons to discuss the public and parliamentary concern about the identified dangers that had come to public attention concerning stage hypnosis. As a result the Home Office Minister Michael Forsythe announced that a review was to be undertaken of the Hypnotism Act 1952. This review was to look into the evidence of possible damage being done to the victims of stage hypnosis used in entertainment. It was also to look at the ways in which those regulations and guidelines were being enforced.

In the preface of that report it said that the review was carried out by a panel of experts from the British Psychological Society and the Royal College of Psychiatrists who, after four meetings, submitted their report to the Minister on 11th October 1995.

The panel members were appointed on the strength of their professional expertise in the evaluation of clinical evidence and research literature. The preface of the report specifically states that "the panel members are not experts in hypnosis". Furthermore "their professional bodies were specifically invited not to nominate anyone with a current involvement in hypnosis, in order to avoid any personal or professional prejudice".

So, if a person is going to have the electrics in their house surveyed, do they call out a plumber, just so they can say it was an impartial consideration?

I don't think so

The British Psychological Society and The Royal College of Psychiatrists, in my opinion, displayed an error of judgement in going along with such a plan. The Home

Office should have contacted the Campaign Against Stage Hypnosis and asked them to make a representation, but they did not and no request was made to CASH to make their knowledge available. Neither was Derek Crussell, the most well-known British hypnotherapist who treats people who have suffered damage from stage hypnosis invited to give an opinion.

The report contained a catalogue of injuries that happened to people during stage hypnosis but in the conclusion these were discounted as not being of great relevance in comparison with the enjoyment of the audience. While there were people identified in the report as having suffered serious and longlasting physical and psychological damage, it jettisoned those people's experiences. Furthermore it specifically said that in comparison with the amount of people involved, the risk factor of damage was low.

References are also made to the panel viewing videos of various television shows about stage hypnosis, but no videography appeared in the report. It must also be considered that any television documentary is ultimately the construction of the director, editor and producer, and not scientific research.

Local authorities were asked to fill in a survey and send it back to the panel; however, many of these bodies cannot always police the performances of stage hypnosis. Although licences for entertainment can be issued by them they usually have no experts to monitor what actually goes on and they rarely have the financial resources to set up such an operation.

The most difficult part of the report for me to accept was a suggestion that there was no comparison of the before and after effects of stage hypnosis in a controlled fashion. As we have seen in this chapter academic hypnotherapy literature is full of references to the after effects that some individuals have suffered, who were quite well before the event. This is also a Chinese loop, because it would be unethical to set up such experiments that would judge the before and after effects of people who were damaged by the process.

From a hypnotherapist's point of view in reading this report, I must question the authors' understanding of the dynamics of hypnosis, intrahypnotic or post-hypnotic suggestions. There was a presupposition that many of the people that suffer injuries have pre-existing problems before the show, but my research shows that is not so. In fact all of the subjects I studied had no pre-existing contraindications to hypnosis.

The report did, however, identify that the participants involved in stage hypnosis were not aware of any risks before, during or after the event. A recommendation was made that the public be warned about the risks involved prior to the show. In its conclusion the report talks about how many of the accidents can be avoided by the hypnotist sticking to the guidelines offered by the government.

No mention was made in the report that the panel members did any field work to see what was really happening on the stage hypnosis circuit. When was the last time they saw a stage hypnosis show in a pub in the East End on a Saturday night?

An anomaly arises when one considers that both the British Psychological Society and Royal College of Psychiatrists are both special institutional members of the United Kingdom Council of Psychotherapy. The members of the Home Office panel were BPS and RCP practitioners. The UKCP strictly prohibits its members from partaking in stage hypnosis.

Home Office Circular no 39/1996: Stage Hypnotism: Review of Hypnotism Act 1952

This circular advised local authorities of the outcome of the Home Office review of the Hypnotism Act 1952 and set out revised model conditions. Authorities were encouraged to attach these recommendations to the licences issued for public performances of stage hypnotism.

The document announced that there was no immediate prospect of legislation to amend the 1952 Act on public demonstration of stage hypnosis for entertainment and says that the panel concluded that "there was no serious risk to participants in stage hypnosis, and any risk that does exist is much less significant than that involved in many other activities".

It further goes on to say that any changes in the Act would be subject to opportunities arising for legislation and in such an event "the additional burden or cost...would have to be justified". Then it basically says that the additional cost of changing such legislation may well be a burden.

Quite out of the blue the circular suggests that local authorities outside London might now charge the stage hypnotists a fee for the granting of the licence (this already happens in London itself). There was also a suggestion that there might be good reason to have a central information point for local authorities to contact when checking on applicants for licensing purposes. Any performer that had given cause for concern could then be identified easily.

The circular recognises that there are "no recognised qualifications or organisations in connection with stage hypnosis". Any such bodies that set themselves up as such can presently have no official recognition. The only real required need that the local authority may fulfil is to request details of the stage hypnotist's last three performances to give an indication of experience. No disclosure of the contents of the proposed performance is required.

A total lack of the understanding of age regression is put forward when the document states: " A hypnotist may often ask volunteers to behave as if they were a child: this is not age regression." There is a very real danger that because the stage hypnotist has neither the time nor the surroundings to take sufficient care with this procedure, it will, indeed, constitute age regression. On this point an open letter was written to the Home Secretary, by Michael Joseph and appeared in the *European Journal of Clinical Hypnosis*, in the spring of 1997.

Incongruities arise when in one section of the report it says that the hypnotist cannot administer noxious harmful substances nor make any suggestions which could cause anxiety, harm or distress. However, it does not say that the suggestion of noxious substances are prohibited. It goes on to say that "in practice volunteers do not react as if they truly believe that there is, for example, a giant spider behind them, or a bomb under their chair". How can they possibly know how another person will react? Once again a sheer ignorance of the dynamics of hypnosis is displayed.

Another part of the circular says that the hypnotist shall not use selection techniques to coerce suggestible members of the audience to come up on stage. Obviously the writers of this document have never seen a stage hypnotist get everyone on stage and then dismiss the ones who do not respond to their selection procedures, which are fundamental to the success of the hypnotist's show.

A prohibition is placed on the stage hypnotist not to use suggestions that imply the loss of body parts. What the writers again do not seem to understand is that this is easily circumnavigated by turning the suggestion into the growth or reduction of body parts, to whatever size the hypnotist wants.

The final straw that breaks the camel's back is that the circular states that the hypnotist must stay behind for 30 minutes after the show to make sure that none of the subjects are having adverse effects. For the majority of people who suffer adverse reactions to stage hypnosis these problems can often happen well beyond 30 minutes after the show. And why, if the assessed risk is so minimal, would this be necessary at all?

9

The Interviews

Derek Crussell: November 1997

Derek Crussell is a practising hypnotherapist in Bromley, South London and is an active member of CASH. He is widely known as being Britain's leading expert on treating people who purport to suffer from side effects of stage hypnosis.

TOK: How long have you been practising hypnosis?

DC: I've been practising hypnosis for over 40 years, but of course I was not treating people to begin with. I was helping people when I lived in India — I lived there for 18 years you know. In those days I did not charge any money because I had a full-time job doing something else. I set up my practice when I came back here to Bromley over 20 years ago.

TOK: Was there any stage hypnosis in India?

DC: Not very often, but sometimes you would get the odd show, mainly by travelling English-speaking stage hypnotists, but just occasionally a native Indian.

TOK: When did you first encounter stage hypnosis?

DC: Well, that would be around 1950 when the American stage hypnotist Ralph Slater came over here to England. Then of course there was his court case, which resulted in the Hypnotism Act of 1952.

Then Westminster council gave a licence to Andrew Newton to practise stage hypnosis again in the 1980s. At the time I, Dr Waxman and Leo Abse, the Welsh Member of Parliament spoke out against it, warning what would happen.

I then remember being on a television show about stage hypnosis with Margaret Harper in 1994 and she was talking about her daughter who died after a stage hypnosis show. This is when public awareness rose again.

TOK: Tell me about your involvement with CASH?

DC: It's not an organisation that has any members; anyone can join — there are no fees involved, even a next-door neighbour can help out. After meeting Margaret Harper I've tried to help her with all the technical information about hypnosis, and we have had several thousands of people contacting us over the years. Most of them don't want to come forward though; that's one of the tragedies. The majority of people feel they have been through enough and don't want to get involved in court cases or are afraid of being bothered by newspapers.

TOK: How many people have actually come forward?

DC: I've treated 19 people now, who have suffered badly after they had been volunteers in stage hypnosis shows. There have been other people who have lived too far away to come for treatment or for me to visit them.

TOK: Tell me a little more about the kind of lobbying CASH does.

DC: We collect press articles, monitor the news, write to the newspapers and Members of Parliament. Generally we give out information to decision makers, who hopefully may begin to see how dangerous stage hypnosis is.

TOK: Are the problems that victims present similar, or are they very different and diverse?

DC: Very similar. They follow very similar patterns of

behaviours, trauma, confusion, giddyness, headaches, panic attacks, lack of confidence. People are often unable to go to work and end up reporting sick. Some have become long-term sick, after having led seemingly quite normal lives previous to the stage hypnosis.

You see, what happens is that they are sometimes given many different bizarre things to do while they are in deep trance, quickly and one after the other. Due to the circumstances there is an overbearing pressure for them to perform these tasks and for some people it is just too much.

TOK: What do you think the way forward is?

DC: For England it must be to keep badgering the Home Office until they agree to review the guidelines once again, on stage hypnosis and ban it, because the last review they did was nothing less than a disaster. I'm absolutely convinced it is a highly dangerous practice. Think about it, the stage hypnotist actually knows nothing about the volunteer before they hypnotise them. If a professional in the caring sector did that they would be struck off whatever register they were on.

There are no doubts in my mind that Sharron Tabarn died as a result of the effects of stage hypnosis. I've reviewed all the papers, and in my opinion, it seems the only logical reason for such a healthy woman to die in the circumstances she did.

TOK: What advice would you give to anyone who thinks they might have been damaged by being a volunteer in a stage hypnosis show?

DC: I would say to them come forward let us help you. In the majority of cases, in time, people can get better. There is no need to suffer in silence; help is at hand. After all it would be the price of a phone call, just to telephone us for advice. Of course everything they tell us is in the strictest of confidence.

And if then they want to go on and sue the cowboy who did it to them we will help them with the legal matters too. Some people have even been awarded legal aid and there are presently four cases going through the courts as we speak.

What we would like people to do is contact us and remember that they are not alone.

TOK: What kind of treatment do you use with the victims?

DC: It is different for everyone because no two people or their experiences are the same. Generally I help them to put the trauma to the back of their minds, that is not to forget it completely, because if they want to remember it they can. I also use the installation of positive thoughts to replace the unwanted feelings. It's good to help people feel calmer, more relaxed, peaceful and help build up their confidence again.

TOK: Do you regress them back to the stage show?

DC: No! I never use regression with these people; after all, they have been through enough. One person I'm treating does suffer quite bad flashbacks, but generally it's more a sense of not being able to shake off what has happened to them. Many of them are afraid of hypnosis after their traumatic experiences, so I am also very cautious around that too. It's all taken at a very easy pace. No rush. No hurry. I'm quite a nice chap really you know.

TOK: Is there anything you would like to add to what you have said?

DC: Well, you know this has all got out of hand the past few years. Since Paul McKenna got his television show, stage hypnosis has become a craze again. Lots of chaps that were out of work saw stage shows and thought to themselves: "I can do that and it's better than staying on welfare." Before long all sorts of untrained and inexperienced people were doing stage hypnosis shows in almost every pub around the country.

First they started charging £20 a show, then £50 and then a great deal more. Suddenly, a few years ago, if a pub didn't have a least one night a week of stage hypnosis, it wasn't a pub. Performing a stage hypnosis show is not hard. Anyone can do it, with a little bit of knowledge that they could learn in a few hours, but these people have no idea about the consequences of their actions. They have not studied the human mind or any kind of therapy. It's not like a juggler putting the balls back in the box at the end of the night. These are real people's lives they are messing around with.

With CASH, our experience has shown that the volunteers do not have to be doing over-the-top things for them to be damaged. It is often the quiet ones in the show who may have been instructed to do quite mundane things, but the stage hypnotist is never going to see that person again and does not know what will happen to them.

As for FESH, at one stage it only had a handful of members. I remember when Peter Casson was alive and the president; he told me he would only have the most experienced stage hypnotists as members, although I disputed there was no such thing.

The report by the panel members reviewing the guidelines for stage hypnosis says that a stage hypnotist must stay behind for 30 minutes after the show to ensure that everyone is all right, but that would not make a blind bit of difference. All the people I have seen have developed problems more than an hour later, the next day, after a week or sometimes longer.

The only solution is to have the performance of stage hypnosis as an entertainment made illegal because there are too many dangerous variables in the whole procedure and the public ought to be protected.

Margaret Harper: November 1997
Founder of CASH
Margaret is the mother of Sharron Tabarn, who died after

a stage hypnosis show, in my opinion, of a heart attack, after having reacted to the suggestion that 10,000 volts of electricity would go through her body.

TOK: Who first started CASH?

MH: I first started CASH on 1st January 1994 with my husband Kevin, my daughter Collette, and Collette's boyfriend at the time, Gordon. We had all been unhappy with the inquest's verdict on my daughter's death, so we decided to try and do something about it.

TOK: What did the campaign set out to achieve?

MH: The purpose of the group was to try and draw the public's attention to the dangers that can arise from stage hypnotism and to try and get it banned altogether in England. Obviously the people who are taking part are unaware of the dangers that can arise and due to our own experience we thought we ought to set out to warn them. It is not everyone who could be damaged by it, but there are links with side effects suffered by some people after they have undergone stage hypnosis.

TOK: How is the campaign financed?

MH: The campaign is financed by myself. I have been working two nights a week in a nursing home and that has brought in £70 a week, but now I am going to take on more child minding to support the campaign.

TOK: So you are supporting the campaign on your own?

MH: Yes and Gordon also donated a fax, typewriter and lots of stationery.

TOK: What kind of support has the campaign had?

MH: The local press have been a great support. They have been wonderful at getting the information out to the public. I think without them we wouldn't have got as far as we have. Yes, they have been a huge help and of course then the daily papers picked it up and ran many articles. We feel we have a lot to thank the press for in helping us.

Right at the beginning we also contacted Colin Pickthall, our MP and he initiated the adjournment debate in the House of Commons in 1994, which prompted the government's review.

Then the television companies heard what was going on and we got air time on various debates and chat shows, where I came across many other people who had been damaged by stage hypnosis.

TOK: What was your reaction to the results of the review on stage hypnosis?

MH: We were very shocked that on the review panel they had people who had no specialist knowledge of hypnosis. Therefore they found very little evidence that there was any danger to the public, but we feel these were not the correct people to have had sitting on that panel. We only found this out after we received the review paper and it said the panel had no specialist knowledge of hypnosis.

We were horrified and sent a letter back questioning the review. It seemed contradictory, because if there were no dangers, why have a Hypnotism Act at all?

TOK: Did you get a reaction from the letter you sent in?

MH: Yes, we got a quick, sharp letter back, which said very little. They did, of course, change some of the things in the 1952 Hypnotism Act, after the review, stating that certain suggestions should not be made, particularly harmful ones. However, that's nonsense because who knows what is in a stranger's mind and what they may perceive as being harmful?

TOK: How has the campaign's role developed?

MH: Apart from supporting the victims we have had local authorities contacting us, asking for advice on the dangers of stage hypnosis. Now many more of them, after talking to the campaign, have prohibited stage hypnosis in their areas. We have also been invited along to council meetings and many of them have come to the conclusion that they will not permit shows.

TOK: What do you think will happen now?

MH: Stage hypnosis is already getting much less popular and the prohibitions are being put in place by local authorities, many of whom think the government review was just ridiculous. Of course governments don't like to be seen banning anything unless it's very high profile and means votes.

We have also had support and communications from abroad: America, Australia, India, Italy. This is often because many of the English stage hypnotists are going to these places to perform.

TOK: How is your daughter's case going?

MH: We have now been granted legal aid and have been given permission by the attorney general to seek to re-open the case and get the inquest heard in the High Court. After great discussion the crime that we think should be levelled at the stage hypnotist is one of unlawful killing.

Stage Hypnotist Tony Padgett: August 1997
As I was finishing the final preparations for this book I got an e-mail from Tony, who agreed to communicate with me and gave permission for our communications to appear in this book.

TP: I just viewed your web page and discovered that you are writing a book about the "terrible practices of stage hypnosis" and the "terrible effects some volunteers have suffered" because of stage hypnotism. I have been performing stage hypnotism for 10 years. I have hypnotised thousands of people, and have always been told by the volunteers that it is a wonderful experience. The worst complaint that I ever got was a bit of a stiff neck or headache, due to their head leaning forward for a long period of time, which I try to remedy during the show.

Out of curiosity, could you please give me a few examples that you ran across about the terrible effects of stage hypnotism? It would help me in my continuous study of hypnotism in general. It would also prepare me for any potential trouble that someone might encounter, although, I can't imagine anything seriously bad coming from my show, since I pay extremely close attention to my volunteers and treat them with the utmost respect while they explore their own images and minds.

TOK: I will be happy to enter into discourse with you, but first of all please provide me with details of your training in the application of hypnosis, qualifications, professional memberships, business address, telephone number and permission to use all communications in my publication. If you are sure you are right you will have no objection to providing the aforementioned details.

TP: Several seminars in hypnosis and NLP including those of Charlie Badenhop here in Japan and Dr Steven Gilligan. Qualifications: I have taught basic courses in the USA and Japan since 1988. Training includes history of hypnosis; level of trance; pre-induction; induction; deepening; suggestion structure; self-relational Work; anchoring; quotes; metaphors; indirect trance phrases; I have been doing shows since 1987 with great success and I started doing shows in Japan this year.

Professional memberships: president and founder of the Hypnosis Society of Miami University (Ohio) 1988-89; president and founder of the Hypnosis Society of the American Graduate School of International Management 1989-90; president and founder of the Hypnosis Society of Japan. You have my permission to use our communications in your publication.

TOK: Of all your trainings and hypnosis experiences you mention no recognised certifications. Are you a member of the American Psychological Association, American Medical Association, American Psychiatric Association, or any equivalent body? You have mentioned training with Steven Gilligan, PhD from Stanford University; however, since Gilligan writes on Ericksonian training in hypnosis, it must be remembered that Erickson was a psychiatrist who did not permit stage hypnotists on his courses. Erickson further helped found the American Society of Clinical Hypnosis, which believes stage hypnosis should be prohibited by law.

Neither do you mention whether any of the associations that you belong to are recognised by any of the bodies above.

After all, I have sat at the controls of a passenger plane while it is crossing the Atlantic, but that does not make me a qualified pilot. Of course I could form an association and call it the Transatlantic Association of Aviation and declare myself the president.

Since you are an American practising hypnosis, unaware of the complications that may arise through stage hypnosis, I ask you to comment on the work of Frank J MacHovec: *Hypnosis Complications: Prevention and Risk* (1986).

TP: No, I did not know that hypnotists needed such certification? Is that a law? If so, please let me know. I have only heard of two states in the USA having some type of certification but that does not include stage hypnosis, and I am currently in Japan, and Japan has no such laws.

I did attend Dr Gilligan's seminar and enjoyed talking with him. I was invited by my mentor, Charlie Badenhhop, and at no time was I asked what type of hypnosis I practised. And as for Milton Erickson, I've studied a bit of his work. Great stuff. I never did read anywhere he says that stage hypnosis should be outlawed. If there is such controversy, why is it not outlawed? I think Erickson's works are great but I don't agree with him if he did say such a thing.

All the associations I belong to are self-study groups. Do they need to belong to any of the others you mentioned?

What I am doing is not clinical or therapeutic hypnosis; it's people enjoying their own imaginations. I do not "scare" people into trance, which I have seen others do. My techniques are very open and natural — very close to what Ericksonian hypnotists would probably use. Do you have anything against a good storyteller leading you on a relaxing, intriguing journey?

TOK: Ericksonian Hypnosis is nothing like what a stage hypnotist does, and to suggest such a thing displays a complete misunderstanding of Erickson's work.

TP: Fair enough, I will look at MacHovec. I am just wondering why all the questions about my background? As a person who is trying to stop all the "terrible things that happen" with stage hypnosis, it would seem that you would want to discuss the issues rather than my background.

I am sure you are familiar with Ormond McGill. He wrote several books on stage hypnosis and I have read all of them. Not once did he mention any adverse reactions to stage hypnosis, and he is considered the "Dean of American Hypnotists". So are you against stage hypnosis in general, or just bad hypnotists? I would agree if you chose the latter, but I cannot imagine why you would want to ban the former.

TOK: So you think people should be allowed to practise without any kind of certification?

TP: So do you think that a good storyteller needs certification to tell a story? Look, when I'm on stage performing "hypnosis", I am aiding people to explore their own minds. I don't think we're talking about therapy here. I am not asking them to regress to age six and relive their most traumatic experiences. I'm asking them to use their imaginations to explore what it would be like to be a ballet dancer, an alien, a drunk, etc. I've never, ever been told that it was a bad experience. Never once. On the contrary, those who have talked to me afterwards have said it's the best "trip" they've ever had.

As for certification, I'm sure that the "bad" stage hypnotists will be weeded out by natural selection. People can tell the difference. I've seen other hypnotists with both rotten "bad" vibes and with "good" vibes. And the more qualifications a good hypnotist has, the more he or she will be in demand and the other bad ones will be left behind. Same goes for a magician, doctor, dentist, singer, etc.

Anyway I believe I have enough experiences and have taken enough workshops and seminars to qualify as a good, solid stage hypnotist and as a hypnotist in general. However, I don't practise therapy because I don't believe I have the experience to do so. I only let people experience trance. What they do with it is their own business.

TOK: Milton Erickson stated that he believed that a person who practises hypnosis should have training as a healthcare professional.

TP: Again, I love Erickson's work but I don't have to agree with everything he said. He is not the only authority on hypnosis. Shall we conjure up Anton Mesmer's thoughts?

And I wasn't banned from Dr Gilligan's seminars and have done several workshops here with a prominent NLP trainer in Japan (Charlie Badenhop). Are you saying that since I was able to join their trainings, workshops and seminars, they don't practise Ericksonian hypnosis? By the way have you ever met Steven Gilligan? He is a very gentle and caring man.

And hold on a minute, you have never seen my work. How can you make a judgement of my performance and understanding of Ericksonian hypnosis? Are you saying that I don't use binds, double binds, metaphor, quotes, time distortion, confusion, etc? If you were to go through

2

Hypnotic Realities by Erickson and look at my show you
would see similarities. However my purpose is for exploration and fun and not therapy. That's the difference.

TOK: So you are telling me that you have been a practising American hypnotist for all these years and never read
your own country's most prestigious work on possible
complications with hypnosis (MacHovec)?

TP: I didn't know that this was a requirement. There are
people in the USA who have never read the Constitution,
the Declaration of Independence, the Bill of Rights. Does
that mean that they are not US citizens?

TOK: I am familiar with McGill's work. He did say, however, that the American Medical Association is of the opinion
that stage hypnosis should be prohibited. Why do you
think that is?

TP: Exactly what page was it that he said stage hypnosis
should be prohibited. I have the book and I can't see to
find it. Also if it is their opinion that it should be prohibited and it is not, why do you think that is? And why would
a person active in stage hypnosis want to say that his own
profession be banned? Why do you think that is?

TOK: Do you really believe that you can cancel all of your
post-hypnotic suggestions?

TP: Well, I can only suggest to them so it's up to them how
they interpret it. Just the same as how they interpret some
of my suggestions. But let me ask you this, what type of
suggestions are harmful that I use? I will list them here for
your reference: fishing; going cold and hot; laughing; name
stuck in throat; name changed; zipper/bra unsnaps;
nakedness (both volunteers and audience); I become invisible; favourite body parts become 10 times larger; men
become pregnant; becoming an orchestra conductor,
alien, translator, ballet dancer; bad smell; and some oth-

ers that escape me at the moment. Anyway tell me, what "terrible" things could possibly come from these?

TOK: What medical and psychological histories do you take from your subjects?

TP: I screen my volunteers as I induce trance to see any abnormal reactions (crying, unusual swaying, unusual catalepsy, abnormal increased breathing, sweating, change in skin colour/tone, their expressions, etc).

Anyway how many medical and psychological histories are taken from people who go and see an exciting movie, or go to an amusement park, or enter into a romantic relationship?

A final note

At the time of going to press I received a fax from a Canadian stage hypnotist called Attila J Kun, who said that he had performed over one hundred shows in 1997 and besides that he was a "certified clinical hypnotherapist". Kun said he had noticed a succession of amateur stage hypnotists who had appeared in Alberta lately and he had compiled a list of almost 40 people. The most interesting quote in his fax was: "The results of untrained amateurs performing hypnosis shows could lead to *unintentional emotional, sexual, physical and psychological abuse*".

10

Conclusion

NLP

Since the early 1970s a new renaissance in hypnosis commenced again, largely through the rejection of chemical medicine and the development of Neuro-Linguistic Programming (NLP), a discipline of hypnotic counselling techniques. After a century of the intense pursuit of allopathic cure-alls, it has become evident that our partial abandonment of philosophical healing has greatly been to our detriment. The popularisation of hypnosis in hypnotherapy, medicine, dentistry, psychology, psychiatry, psychotherapy and education has been a move back towards personal-centred healing and self-actualisation.

One of the founders of NLP once said that it allowed practitioners to use hypnosis where it had not been used before and had previously encountered hostility. NLP grew very rapidly as a discipline in the 1970s, because it was able to make behavioural changes swiftly and effectively without the old image problem of hypnosis derived from years of the felonious mysticism of stage hypnosis.

In the Autumn 1996 edition of *Rapport*, the English magazine for NLP practitioners, Gordon Ellis, a therapist, wrote about how he sees that there is a need for this discipline to grow beyond its process-only based roots. Ellis, having studied philosophy and Buddhism, seems to explore the idea that while the very essence of NLP was to find a set of mechanical processes that related only to each individual client, it seems now to have gone too far in that direction.

Since NLP is used in the business world, this begs the question of the values and appropriateness of using hypnotic techniques in order to sell and manipulate work forces. This almost schizophrenic discipline is now beginning to split off into two distinct factions: one relevant to the business world and the other the application of NLP techniques for psychotherapeutic uses.

While it is true that the absolutism of overbearing authority frequently tries to impose sociological, moral or religious models of behaviour on the individual, it is not a sensible move to encourage hypnotists to practise without a sound grounding in a caring profession.

Can practising hypnosis without the hypnotist considering moral and value based judgements be safe for the public?

What if a person presents themselves to a hypnotist and declares that they wish to be the best business person they can, and if that means trampling on other people, so what?

Is the hypnotist obliged to assist the client to achieve their identified goal without offering some moral guidance?

Does this discourse make me sound like an advocate of morality, or sound like the imposition of the will of the hypnotist on the unsuspecting subject?

Well, perhaps that might be true, if my model of the world were to be moral, and it is, because all our models of the world are moral, according to our own individual codes. But just because I may believe, as a therapist, that the will of authority, whatever authority, should not be imposed upon the individual, it does not mean that hypnotic subjects never need guidance.

The application of hypnosis is a strong tool that can be used to alter human behaviour dramatically, just the same as drugs or profound cognitive behaviour techniques. Each are instruments of creativity, exploration and healing, and need to be handled with care in order to gain the most benefit to the patient, client or subject. Inept, careless or slapdash application can cause physical, mental, spiritual and sociological distress.

In the Winter 1996 issue of *Rapport*, Ellis again talks about NLP needing to grow beyond its roots to find a spiritual element. He believes people should not be used or manipulated. Not everyone who works in this discipline would agree with him, for some of them believe that in no way should the morality of the hypnotist be imposed upon the client's map of the world.

The ability of a hypnotist to alter the behaviour of an individual through minimalist or expansionist hypnosis goes far beyond the comprehension of the layperson. As hypnotists we are hypnotising people constantly, out of their conscious awareness, changing their behaviour without their conscious knowledge. This is, the majority of the time, justified as a precise behavioural technique to help people become well or actualised and to improve the quality of their lives.

However, for the hypnotist who possesses this knowledge, the questions of morality and responsibility must remain constantly in their mind. Otherwise, what can be a tool of human excellence becomes a cudgel of coercive manipulation to be used by those who wish to benefit from the misfortunes of others.

Hypnosis is a fast track gateway to the unconscious mind, which can unleash a complex set of psychological and physiological effects. Almost 99% of the time these are safe and absorbed into the personality's coping mechanism, but the other 1% of people need the extra guidance of a highly trained hypnotist to pay particular attention to that individual. This can never happen in stage hypnosis, firstly because the stage hypnotist is not sufficiently trained, secondly because circumstances do not allow, and thirdly because the subject is under pressure to perform and not pay attention to their own needs.

Concepts of pain and suffering
The ultimate question that this book asks is:

Is the stage hypnotist responsible for the perceived pain and suffering of the subject, who experiences adverse effects after stage hypnosis?

In order to address this question, we must look at the

interperatation of pain, suffering and distress, and such an enquiry can prove to be a Pandora's box. All perceptions of such subjective experience not only differ from culture to culture, person to person but must also be based in each singular experience, which may alter with the passage of time.

A hurt thumb to a child may seem monumental, but the same experience to an adult may be less traumatic, and the very same disturbance to a soldier in battle might even be inconsequential. The fact that the hurt thumb may be happening to the same person during different times, places and circumstances changes the perception of such an experience.

Is that distressed thumb mainly the result of a physical damage to the body or the perception arrived at through psychosomatic interpretation? Can the validity of either equation be diminished by the fact that the same experience would be perceived as less or more traumatic by a different person, under other circumstances, somewhere else, at another time?

Therefore, is the stage hypnotist responsible for the extraordinary physical, mental, social and spiritual processes happening within the subject prior to, during or after the stage performance?

These questions are constantly being asked in the clinical and experimental practice of hypnosis, but the stage hypnotist denies that such enquiries are their responsibility. They are performers and that is both their identity and their profession. They do not consider that what is or may be happening to their volunteers, outside of the stage hypnosis, is any of their business.

Herein lies the fundamental flaw of stage hypnosis for entertainment purposes: it concentrates solely on a small portion of the volunteers' life circumstances, not taking into account and denying responsibility for the whole picture.

Clinical, experimental and demonstration hypnosis
Such deliberation now begs the question as to why the

experimental and clinical hypnotist does not undergo the same circumstantial blindness for their subjects' whole human condition.

To deny that never happens would be foolhardy, because even in the clinic or laboratory the hypnotist is always working with a subject, of whom they have only a limited knowledge. No hypnotist can ever know everything about their subjects, but the basic knowledge of the subject, gathered by a clinical or experimental hypnotist, is far superior in quantity and quality than the mere cursory attention that the stage hypnotist pays to their volunteers.

The stage hypnotists may protest that demonstration hypnosis neither has the time nor luxury afforded to the clinic or laboratory. They would, of course, be right, as a person stepping up to volunteer during a professional demonstration of hypnosis may be unknown to the hypnotist. However, the objectives of the demonstration hypnotist are different to those of the stage hypnotist. It is the goal of the demonstration hypnotist to inform the audience about hypnotic phenomena that occur during hypnosis, or to demonstrate physiological, mental or spiritual change.

For the demonstration hypnotist, the presupposition that the volunteers' welfare must be of paramount importance is above the successful demonstration of hypnosis. So if we support demonstration hypnosis, are we then saying that hypnosis can be carried out safely, without the subject having had an extensive preliminary interview with the hypnotist?

The answer to that question would be a resounding "yes", since all hypnotists use hypnosis with subjects in the first waking state of trance, not having utilised a formal induction. The dividing line between the use of waking suggestion and hypnotic manipulation, at this point, is context-bound.

Furthermore the ethics of the experimental use of hypnosis in the laboratory teeter on a precarious and exposed high wire. Is it less moral to use hypnosis to entertain and make people laugh than it is to experiment on human beings by testing their thresholds to pain?

Indeed there are times in experimental hypnosis, in a laboratory, when the scientific exploration of knowledge temporarily overtakes the good of the subjects. If the subject has volunteered to suffer excruciating pain, while under hypnosis, does that then allow the hypnotist to contravene ethical applications of hypnosis?

Looking at these considerations a crack appears in the unity between clinical and experimental hypnotists as they split off into their separate groups; one the healer, one the experimenter.

To complicate the matters more, when the use of forensic hypnosis rears its head, with the FBI, CIA, MI5, KGB and numerous other legal and illegal government operations, the abuse in stage hypnosis suddenly pales into insignificance.

In pastoral ministering hypnosis also stands the chance of being abusive when used by self-made prophets who entrance their subjects in the name of God. As I write this book, an evangelical lay preacher has just held services in the church across the road. During the service I observed, his flock of bedazzled and vulnerable lambs were hypnotised and then given post-hypnotic suggestions for healing a kaleidoscope of ailments and woes. Of course he did not call it hypnosis, but as a hypnotist, I certainly did. The truth was, he was not very good and his failures were high, but without a doubt it was hypnosis and he knew it.

The use of hypnosis in education also does not give the circumstantial safety afforded to the hypnotised subject outside the clincial setting, but under those circumstances only light hypnosis is usually used.

Gurus

Let us for a while now consider the kind of status that the stage hypnotists can attain in the public eye through their own good publicity machines, and in doing this it is important to remember that we are discussing hypnotists who work with mass suggestion. The psychiatrist Anthony Storr, in his book *Feet of Clay: A Study of Gurus* looks at individuals who have high levels of communication skills and can get followers to do just about anything.

Many people are suggestible, vulnerable and looking for someone else to point out a direction for them to go. It does not always matter whether that direction is logical or in their interests, because sometimes they want the relief of resuming the role of the child again, allowing others to make the decisions for them.

Public hypnotists can move to guru status, as Erickson did within clinical hypnosis, Spanos in experimental hypnosis, and McGill in stage hypnosis. In psychiatry Laing became a guru, likewise Freud within psychotherapy, and Charcot in neurology. Some of the work of the theorists remain in tact with time, and some decay.

However, there are those who achieve such exalted, unquestionable public image who exhibit psychotic characteristics such as Hitler, Mussolini, Stalin, Ceausescu, or Mao Tse-Tung. People like Jim Jones or David Koresh dominate cults, leading people to set up belief systems that turn them into automatons, who will obey, even to the point of murder and mass suicides.

It would not be fair to say that these individuals may have been psychotic to begin with, because they often initially strived for noble causes, but later they became detached from their original intentions. They became disassociated and unable to judge the undertones and feedback of public consciousness.

I am not saying that all stage hypnotists are psychotics or gurus or leaders, but such status afforded to an individual often leads them to believe their own publicity, disregarding criticism and unopen to debate.

Storr also talks about confidence tricksters often being misclassified as being saner than they are. He believes that they are often more abnormal than those who prosecute or define them realise. I would classify some stage hypnotists as confidence tricksters and not as professional hypnotists, because their skills are limited. They have rarely sought education or qualifications in the field of hypnosis, failing to study, beyond a reasonable level, that which would more than likely ensure their subject's safe-

ty. They generally do not seek to further the field of hypnosis, but simply to exploit it for their own personal financial gain.

The EJCH affair

In the spring of 1996 I spotted an article in the *European
Journal of Clinical Hypnosis*, to which I am a subscriber,
which reviewed a course run by Paul McKenna, the stage
hypnotist, and his business partner. The article was written by a Scottish psychologist who had attended the
course and extolled its virtues.

The journal specifically states, at the back, under its
editorial policy, that it does not promote stage hypnosis for
entertainment. I also knew that Michael Joseph, the owner
of the journal, was strongly opposed to the practice of
stage hypnosis for entertainment, believing it to be dangerous. This is why I was so surprised to see the article
promoting the course of a hypnotist who was so publicly
involved with stage hypnosis.

Objecting to this indirect promotion of McKenna's stage
hypnosis activities, I wrote in a letter detailing one of his
shows I had seen, and it was duly published.

Immediately after that I received many telephone calls
from clinical hypnotists saying how they agreed with me.
Some were heads of training establishments and the consensus of opinion was that it was about time someone
started to write more publicly about this kind of hypnotic
abuse.

I even got a letter from a practitioner as far away as
Mumbia in India, who wrote to me, expressing his support
for my objections, believing that the use of hypnosis in
entertainment is simply misuse. He said that a person
would not be allowed to use a surgeon's scalpel to entertain, so why should hypnosis be allowed to be used in
such a way.

Although my objections were profound, they were limited to a professional journal, that the public would never
see. A few days later I received a distraught telephone call
from Bill Doult, the editor of the journal, who was very

upset because McKenna had said he would sue. Bill had not slept for three days, after having spoken to McKenna on the telephone. He sounded exhausted and was terrified of losing his house, family and wealth. Shortly afterwards he resigned his post.

Michael Joseph stepped in and offered McKenna a full page right to reply in the journal, but this was refused and a writ for libel was issued against myself, the journal and Michael Joseph. We are not the first to be sued by this man; there were two ongoing court cases against newspapers at this time. However, getting a defence together is a very expensive business, and over the next five months it cost us in excess of £40,000. The journal, in order to survive and pay the legal bills, had to send a plea for financial help out to all its readers and the hypnosis community in general. The response from the profession was good and the journal is still going strong at the time of press.

I found that Michael Joseph was a man of great integrity and was determined to stand his ground. We did not back down, and entered the defence on 13th February 1997. The plaintiff was supposed to reply to our defence within 14 days, but we did not hear back from McKenna's lawyers.

Westminster Council

In 1997 I wrote to the councillor who ran the public entertainment licensing committee in Westminster to complain, both as a professional and resident, about stage hypnosis. Councillor David Chambers quoted the 1996 government review and said that the council had received complaints that their restrictions were unreasonably stringent. He replied: "In my view to completely prohibit stage hypnotism in Westminster would be unreasonable, particularly in view of the Home Office review and circular. What we have sought to do is take all reasonable precautions to protect people who attend performances."

The entertainment newspaper *The Stage*, in January 1997, reported that Westminster Council was lobbying hard to persuade the Home Office to have controls on shows that took place at private parties and clubs. Councillor Alan Bradley, chairman of the council's planning and environment committee, was concerned about hypnosis shows taking place in some venues with absolutely no safeguards whatsoever. John Birchall of FESH commented: "If you start to license any private entertainment it's an infringement of people's civil liberties".

The Law
The civil right and liberty to practise hypnosis as an alternative form of treatment or therapy is enshrined in UK common law. It is different from Napoleonic law in that it seeks protect the right to practise alternative medicine, instead of seeking to protect the individual from exploitation. Common law can only control the practice of hypnosis as a therapy when it becomes accepted and registered with the government and so far that has not happened to hypnosis.

Since the arrival in the West of Maharishi Mahesh Yogi, who was popularised by his connection to the Beatles, the dividing lines between altered states of awareness have blurred. Deepak Chopra today promotes his form of Ayurveda meditation, which begs the question of what is mediation and what is trance. To consider and quantify trance is ultimately an ideological impossibility, but to identify what we might consider as being deep somnambulistic trance-like behaviour can only be assessed by professional hypnotists themselves.

Unfortunately the continuity of training in the application of hypnosis all over the world leaves a lot to be desired, with some schools not coming up to what might be considered a reasonable standard. These often include courses that teach hypnosis to practitioners of medicine, psychology, psychotherapy as well as hypnotherapy. However, this is changing as hypnotherapy itself establishes BAs, MAs and doctorates in hypnosis.

By far the majority of courses teach that hypnosis should never be used for entertainment. The loophole arises when we consider that most of these establishments are private and do not want to dent their profit margins by being involved in a public battle over the issue of stage hypnosis.

Since hypnotists themselves have generally failed to implement the kind of standards that would ensure, as much as possible, the public's safety, governments must ultimately be held responsible. Of anyone, it should be these professionals, who use hypnosis, who should seek vehemently to police it, since they must ultimately be philosophically responsible for its ethical use. It is these well-qualified hypnotists who should all be strongly lobbying the governments to implement their recommendations, but often they do not.

Many professionals bang the drum of injustice, only when it suits their own personal gains, and not in order to protect the public. Perhaps having read this work they will use some of that hypnosis to motivate themselves into joining CASH or its equivalent, both as singular and institutional members. They would be welcomed and honoured for their efforts.

As Britain goes into Europe a plethora of committees and sub-committees are in constant negotiations with various hypnosis organisations, quantifying, qualifying, and attempting to regulate and restrict the practice of hypnosis. It is possible that at some point stage hypnosis will be prohibited in Britain, as it is in parts of Europe, prosecuting those involved for practising medicine illegally. However, this is not guaranteed, because in Spain you cannot practise hypnosis for therapy unless you are a medical doctor. Yet they allow stage hypnosis?

What is and what is not hypnosis is obviously going to be quite a large problem to define, if a complete ban on hypnosis for entertainment ever comes into play in England. In Switzerland autogenics became hypnosis by another name and in Spain sophrology did exactly the same thing, making hypnosis indirectly permissible.

However, in some countries like Denmark and France a total ban on stage hypnosis does work successfully and it is most unlikely that any of those countries will be changing their positions in the future. So to say that a ban would not work or would produce an underground of illegal, private stage hypnosis shows is not necessarily true.

Both the British and other governments need to take the responsibility of protecting the general public against the dangers of stage hypnosis. In Britain there most certainly needs to be another Home Office review of the situation and this time it needs to have experts in the field of hypnosis on the panel.

Afterword

On 21st August 1997 the *Daily Telegraph* reported that Carlton Television had dropped the stage hypnotist Paul McKenna and would not be making any more of his hypnotic shows. According to the article the programme received disappointing ratings and critics were apparently less than impressed with the shows.

CASH continues to be held in the hands of a few individuals who are dedicated to the eventual prohibition of stage hypnosis. At times they stand alone without sufficient support, backing or help from many in hypnotherapy, medicine, psychology and the behavioural sciences. In writing and researching this project many distinguished hypnotists simply did not return my calls, not wishing to get involved in anything controversial.

Those who have suffered the side effects of stage hypnosis **can** get professional help, which can greatly aid their recovery and assist them towards leading a full and happy life. At times clinical hypnosis may be the best way of proceeding with that help, but no one would be forced in any way to do anything they did not think was right and proper, or against their interests or wishes.

In the back of this book is a copy of a petition that CASH is using to gather signatures to prohibit stage hypnosis for entertainment purposes.

Please photocopy and use the petition

Join the efforts of CASH
Help us to help the vulnerable stay safe
&
To the stage hypnotists I say:
You can use hypnosis kindly

BIBLIOGRAPHY

ANDREAS, CONNIRAE, PhD, & ANDREAS, STEVE, MA
Heart of the Mind, Real People Press, Utah, USA, 1989.

ASCH, S E
Social Psychology, Englewood Cliffs, Prentice-Hall, New Jersey 1952.

BANDLER, RICHARD & GRINDER, JOHN
Trans-formations, Real People Press, Utah, USA, 1981.

BASS, ELLEN &DAVIS, LAURA
The Courage to Heal, Harper & Row, New York, 1988.

BURROWS, J F (KARLYN)
Secrets of Stage Hypnotism, Stage Electricity and Bloodless Surgery, The Magician Ltd, London 1912.

CANFIELD, JACK & HANSEN, MARK VICTOR
A 2nd Helping of Chicken Soup for the Soul, Health Communications Inc, Florida, 1995.

CHOKROVERTY, SUDHANSU, MD,
Sleep Disorders Medicine, Butterworth-Heinemann, USA, 1994.

CHOPRA, DEEPAK, MD
Quantum Healing, Bantam Books, USA and London, 1989.

CRASILNECK, HAROLD B & HALL, JAMES A
Clinical Hypnosis: Principles & Applications: Second Edition, Allyn & Bacon, USA, 1985.

DILTS, ROBERT, with HALLBOM, TIM & SMITH, SUZI
Beliefs, Metamorphous Press, Oregon, 1990.

ERICKSON, MILTON H, MD
The Collected Papers of Milton H Erickson on Hypnosis: Volumes 1 - 4. Edited by Rossi, Ernest L, Irvington Publishers Inc, New York, 1989.

ERICKSON, MILTON H, MD, & ROSSI, ERNEST L, PhD
The February Man, Brunner/Mazel, New York, 1989.

ERICKSON, MILTON H, MD, ROSSI, ERNEST L, PhD & ROSSI, SHEILA I **Hypnotic Realities**, Irvington Publishers Inc, New York, 1976.

EVANGELISTA, ANITA
Dictionary of Hypnotism, Greenwood Press, Connecticut, 1991.

FROMM, E & SHOR, R E (EDS)
Hypnosis: Developments in Research and New Perspectives: Second Edition, Aldine, Chicago, 1979.

GAULD, ALAN
A History Of Hypnotism, Cambridge University Press, New York, 1992.

GIBSON, H B & HEAP MICHAEL
Hypnosis in Therapy, Lawrence Erlbaum Associates Ltd, Hove, UK, 1991.

GILLIGAN, STEPHEN, PhD,
Therapeutic Trances, Brunner/Mazel, New York, 1987.

GROF, STANISLAV, MD
The Adventure of Self-Discovery, State University of New York Press, Albany, 1988.

HAMMOND, D CORYDON, PhD, (ED)
Hypnotic Inductions & Suggestion: An Introductory Manual, The American Society of Clinical Hypnosis, Des Plaines, 1995.

HAMMOND, D CORYDON, PhD, (ED)
Handbook of Hypnotic Suggestions and Metaphors, an American Society of Clinical Hypnosis book, W W Norton & Co, USA, 1990.

HARDING, H C
Complications Arising from Hypnosis in Entertainment, In: **Hypnosis and its Bicentennial** (Eds Frankel and Zamansky), Plenum, New York, 1978.

HILGARD, ERNEST, & HILGARD, JOSEPHINE
Hypnosis in The Relief of Pain: Revised Edition, Brunner/Mazel, New York, 1994.

HIRSCHBERG, CARYLE AND BARASCH, MARC IAN
Remarkable Recovery, BCA, London and New York, 1995.

KROGER, WILLIAM S, MD
Clinical and Experimental Hypnosis in Medicine, Dentistry and Psychology: Second Edition, J B Lippincott Company, USA 1977.

LUSTIC, DAVID J (LA VELLMA)
Vaudeville Hypnotism, La Vellma Publications, New York, 1930.

LYNN, STEVEN JAY & RHUE, JUDITH W, (EDS)
Theories of Hypnosis: Current Models and Perspectives, Guilford Press, London, 1991.

MACHOVEC, FRANK J, PhD, ABPH
Hypnosis Complications: Prevention and Risk Management, Charles C Thomas, Illinois, 1986.

McKENNA, PAUL
The Hypnotic World of Paul McKenna, Faber and Faber, London, 1993.

McGILL, ORMOND
The New Encyclopedia of Stage Hypnotism, The Anglo American Book Company, Camarthen, 1996.

MILGRAM, S
Obedience To Authority: An Experimental View, Harper & Row, New York, 1974.

RIGAUD, MILO
Secrets of Voodoo, City Light Books, 1985.

ROSSI, ERNEST L, PhD
The Psychobiology of Mind-Body Healing, W W Norton & Co, New York, 1993.

SATIR, VIRGINIA
The New Peoplemaking, Science and Behaviour Books, USA, 1988.

SCHEFLIN, ALAN W, LLM, & SHAPIRO, JERROLD LEE, PhD
Trance on Trial, The Guilford Press, New York, 1989.

SIMONTON, O CARL, MD, MATTHEWS-SIMONTON, STEPHANIE, CREIGHTON, JAMES L
Getting Well Again, Bantam Books, USA and London, 1978.

SPANOS, NICHOLAS P
Multiple Identities & False Memories: A Sociocognitive Perspective, American Psychological Association, Washington DC, 1996.

STORR, ANTHONY, MD
Feet of Clay: A Study of Gurus, Harper Collins, London, 1996.

WAXMAN, DAVID, LRCP, MRCS
Hartland's Medical & Dental Hypnosis: Third Edition,

Baillière Tindall, London, 1989.

WOLINSKY, STEPHEN, PHD WITH RYAN, MARGARET O
Trances People Live, The Bramble Company, USA, 1991.

WOOLGER, ROGER J, PhD
Other Lives, Other Selves, Aquarian, London and USA, 1994.

NEWSPAPERS & MAGAZINES

ALEXANDER, JANE
I owe it all to Milton Erickson, *Mail on Saturday*, 22.5.97.

AMIDON, STEPHEN
Peter Casson, *Independent* 28.10.95.

APPLEYARD, BRYAN
Eye to the main trance, *Times* 16.6.87.

BAKER, NICK
Some Entrancing Evening, *Times*, 13.3.91.

BASSETT, KATE
Under the Spell of a Creep, *Electronic Telegraph*, 23.8.97.

Blythe, Chris,
If You Want a Sex Orgy We'll Shut the Doors and Start Right Now, *Sun*, 12.1.94.

Blythe, Chris,
Dirty Trancing, *Sun* 10.12.94.

Boshoff, Alison,
TV drops Hypnotist who lost his Spell, *Daily Telegraph*, 21.8.97.

BRIGGS, HELEN,
My Daughter died after being hypnotised, *The Big Issue*, August 19-25th no 195, London, 1996.

BROOKE, CHRIS
Two Hours Practice and a Room Full of Girls Obeyed My Every Command, *Daily Mail*, 9.11.94.

BURROW, LISA
Blind Date Hypnotist Made Me Have Sex With A Doll! *The People*, 24.12.94.

BURROW, LISA & DAVIES, MURRAY
Topless Women and Plastic Willies...the Filthy Act of Blind Date hypnotist, *The People*, 18.12.94.

CONLAN, TARA
Case Against Hypnotist Over, *The Stage*, 2.10.97.

DAILY EXPRESS, (unknown author and title), 4.3.53.

DAILY TELEGRAPH (Unknown author)
Hypnosis without a music licence costs publican £25 fine, 2.11.78.

DONOHOE, GRAEME
Stage Show Set Me on the Road to Obsession, *The Glaswegian*, 7.8.97.

EVERYBODY'S MAGAZINE (unknown author and title), London, 1953.

FALDING, JOHN
Night Life. An English newspapers clipping (source unknown from the Theatre Museum, Covent Garden), 12.2.76.

FELLOWS, HENRY,
Letter to *The Times*, 27.12.53.

FIELDER, DAN,
The Persuasive Powers of Paul McKenna, *Here's Health*, April 1997.

FOX, KATRINA
Carlton Rejects CASH Claim over McKenna Shows, *The Stage*, 28.8.97.

GARDENER, DAVID
You are Feeling Sleazy: Hypnotist McKenna in Sex Show Row, *News of the World*, 18.2.96.

GRANT, TOM,
Hypnotist to be Sued Again, *Daily Record*, 26.10.88.

GRYLLS, JAMES
I fell Under a Spell, *Daily Mail* 4.11.94.

HADFIELD, GREG
Tragic Tale of a Hypnotised Man Who Now Thinks He is a Child, *Daily Mail*, 14.12.94.

HERBERT, SUSANNAH
Out of Trance and Into Battle, *Sunday Telegraph*, 11.8.91.

KIRKBRIDE, JULIE
Is it Dangerous to Look into this Man's Eyes? *Daily Telegraph*, 14.12.94.

LEWIS-SMITH, VICTOR
Doctor McKenna, I Can Only Presume, *The Mirror*, 26.4.97.

LEWIS-SMITH, VICTOR
A Degree of Arrogance, *The Mirror*, 19.4.97.

LEWIS-SMITH, VICTOR
An Eye for the Main Trance, *Evening Standard*, 17.4.97.

MANCHESTER EVENING NEWS (unknown author)
Oh, Oh, Seven, January 1995.

MERCER, ALISON
New Controls on Private Hypnotism, *The Stage*, 30.1.97.

MCCRUM, ROBERT
The Trancer, *Guardian Weekend*, 1-2 February 1992.

PATRICK, GUY
Hypnotist Made Me Crave Sex with my Tumble Dryer, *Sun*, 20.9.97.

PEARSON, STEVE
Hypnotised DJ Claims Damages, *Rotherham Advertiser*, 6.12.96.

ROGERS, BYRON
Let Them Eat Raw Onions, *Sunday Telegraph*, 13.11.94.

SUN (unknown author)
Mum Of 2 Dies After Stunt By Hypnotist, 9.3.94.

PAPERS

ASCH, S E
Studies of Independence and Conformity: 1. A Minority of One Against a Unanimous Majority, *Psychology Monographs*, 70,(9, Whole No 416), 1956.

British Government Review on Stage Hypnosis: 1995.

BRITISH MEDICAL ASSOCIATION
Medical Use of Hypnotism (Report of a subcommittee appointed by the Psychological Medicine Group committee of the BMA), *British Medical Journal*, Vol 1, p 190, 23.4.55.

CRUSSELL, DEREK
Caught in the Act: The Victims of Stage Hypnosis, *European Journal of Clinical Hypnosis*, issue 10, Vol 3 no 2, issn 1351-1297, 1996.

COE, W C, KOBAYASHI, K, & HOWARD, M L
Experimental and Ethical Problems of Evaluating the Influence of Hypnosis in Anti-Social Conduct, *Journal of Abnormal Psychology* 82, pp 476-482, 1973.

EARLY, L F & LIFSCHUTZ, J E
A Case of Stigmata, Archives of General Psychiatry, 30, 197-200, 1974.

ECHTERLING, LENNIS G & EMMERLING, DAVID A
Impact of Stage Hypnosis, *American Journal of Clinical Hypnosis*, Vol 29, no 3, January 1987.

ELLIS, GORDON
The Chameleon's Conceit Part 2: Towards an Enriched Model of NLP, *Rapport* issue 33, issn 1356-3270, Autumn, 1996.

FOURIE, D P, & LIFSCHITZ, S
Ecosystemic Hypnosis: Ideas and Therapeutic Application, *British Journal of Experimental and Clinical Hypnosis*, 6, 99-107, 1989.

GORHMAN, GRAHAM & STABLES, CHRISTINE
Survey of Personal Stage Hypnotism Experiences, The National College of Hypnotherapy and Psychotherapy, 1995.

HEAP, MICHAEL
Four Victims, *British Journal of Experimental and Clinical Hypnosis*, 2, 60-62, 1984.

HEAP, MICHAEL
A Case of Death Following Stage Hypnosis: Analysis and Implications, University of Sheffield.

Bibliography

HEAP, MICHAEL
The Nature Of Hypnosis, *The Psychologist*, Vol 9 no 11, November 1996.

HILGARD, E R
A Neodissociation Interpretation of Pain Reduction in Hypnosis, *Psychological Review*, 80, 396-411, 1973.

JOSEPH, MICHAEL
Editorial Leader, *European Journal of Clinical Hypnosis* Vol 4 no 1, ISSN 1351-1297, 1997.

JOSEPH, MICHAEL
Dr Paul McKenna, European Journal of Clinical Hypnosis Vol 4 no 2, ISSN 1351-1297, 1997.

JOSEPH, MICHAEL
Dear Home Secretary, *European Journal of Clinical* Hypnosis Vol 4 no 3, ISSN 1351-1297, 1997.

KEBBEL, MARK, PhD
Alternative Theories Of Hypnosis, *The Psychologist*, Vol 10 no 2, February 1997.

KLEINHAUZ, M R
Misuses of Hypnosis: A Medical Emergency and its Treatment, *International Journal of Clinical and Experimental Hypnosis*, 29, 148-161, 1962.

LECHKY, OLGA
Stage Hypnosis Can Have Devastating Effects, the 10th International Congress of Hypnosis and Psychosomatic Medicine, 1985.

LUNT INGRID
Chris Cullen, President 1997/8, *The Psychologist*, Vol 10 No 6, June 1997.

MILNE BRAMWELL, MB

Hypnotism a Humbug: A Reply, York Medical Society, 1892.

MORGAN, DYLAN
The Defensive Persona, *NCP & NCH Journal*, issn 1365-3504, Autumn 1996.

O'KEEFE, TRACIE
Staging an Ethical Protest, *European Journal of Clincial Hypnosis*, issue 10, Vol 3 no 2, issn 1351-1297, 1996.

ORNE, M T & EVANS, F J
Social Control in the Psychological Experiment: Antisocial Behaviour in Hypnosis, *Journal of Personality and Social Psychology*, 1, 189-200, 1965.

SPANOS, N P
Hypnotic Behaviour: A Social Psychological Interpretation of Amnesia, Analgesia and Trance Logic, *Behavior and Brain Sciences*, 9, 489-467, 1986.

STANLEY, ROBB O, PhD
The Protection of the Professional Use of hypnosis: The Need for Legal Controls, *Australian Journal of Clinical & Experimental Hypnosis*, vol 22, 39-51, 1994.

TRAINER, ANGELA
Another Stage in the Developing Career of Paul McKenna? *European Journal of Clinical Hypnosis*, issue 9, Vol 3 no 1, issn 1351-1297, 1995-6.

WAGSTAFF, GRAHAM F
The Problem of Compliance in Hypnosis: A Social Psychological Viewpoint, *Bulletin of the British Society of Experimental and Clinical Hypnosis*, 2,3-5, 1979.

WAGSTAFF, GRAHAM F & NADIA, JAN
Attitudes Towards State and Cognitive-Behavioural Approaches to Hypnotherapy Before and After Hypnotic

Induction, *Contemporary Hypnosis*, Vol 11 no.2, 67-70, 1994.

INTERNET POSTINGS

Re: **Stage Hypnotist**
(Follow Ups)(Post Follow up) (Substance BBS)(FAQ) Posted by James Szeles on June 02, 1995 at 19.37.03: In reply to Stage Hypnotist posted by Ray Thompson on March 31, 1996 at...57% http.//www.he.net/~sustance/bbs/mes-sages/28.html (Size 2.5K).

Re: **Stage Hypnotist**
posted by James Szeles on June 02, 1996 at 19.37.03: I have a serious question to ask. My very good, lifetime friend, Ganine showed signs of depresion. After a few weeks...56% http:..www.he.net/~sustance/bbs/messages/29.html (Size 3.0K).

The dangers of Hypnosis
David L. Brown, ThM
A publication of Logos Communication Consortium, Inc.
P.O. BOX 173, 1994.

Stage Hypnosis is Harming Hypnotherapy
Posted by Mark Casey, 26.9.96.

Follow Up Re: Stage Hypnosis is harming Hypnotherapy
Posted by Richard Bandler, 6.9.96.

Former Lasalle University Chief Gets Five Years
Butch Badon, *The News Banner*, 30.1.97.

The Dangers of Stage Hyopnosis
Several exchanges between Tracie O'Keefe and Tony Padgett by e-mail, July 1997.

VIDEOGRAPHY & FILMS

Kilroy: Stage Hypnotists, BBC, 6.12.94, VHS Code: NBMV627E TX.

Harry the Horny Hypnotist, Medusa Communications & Marketing Ltd, 1995.

Horizon: Hypnosis, BBC, 18.7.67, 16mm Film Code: PL78721, PL83025.

Man Alive Report: Hypnosis, BBC, 7.3.78, VHS Code: VC 191664.

Russell Harty, BBC, 18.3.82, VHS Code: VC 3646.

The Chair: McKenna, BBC, 1997.

The Hypnotic World of Paul McKenna, Part One, Carlton Television, May 1997.

The Hypnotic World of Paul McKenna, Part Two, Carlton Television, May 1997.

The Serpent and the Rainbow, Universal, 1987.

To the Ends of the Earth: Interview with a Zombie, Channel Four, 1997.

LETTERS & DOCUMENTS

ALLEN, D S
Schizophrenia Psychosis After Stage Hypnosis (Letter to the *British Journal of Psychiatry*, 26.4.95).

AHRENSMEYER
The Cowboy Hypnotist (Letter around 1900s in Theatre Musem).

ANDREW (NEE JOHNSON), PATRICIA
Witness statement, 24.9.93.

BRITISH SOCIETY OF MEDICAL AND DENTAL HYPNOSIS
Death of Sharron Tabarn (Letter, 20.1.94).

DEATH CERTIFICATE
Sharron Tabarn, 1993.

HARPER, MARGARET
Affadavit, 27.6.97.

HEAP, MICHAEL
Death of Sharron Tabarn (Letter to Margaret Harper, 23.6.94).

HEAP, MICHAEL
Witness statement, 28.9.93.

KUN, ATTILA
Help to Stop the Sexual, Psychological and Emotional Abuse in Abuse in Stage Hypnosis Shows (Fax to Tracie O'Keefe, November 1997).

McCANN, MICHAEL HOWARD
Coroner's Report, 1993.

MEDICAL RECORDS
Sharron Tabarn, 1993.

SAVE, RAVI
European Journal Of Clinical Hypnosis Affair (Letter from hypnosis practitioner in India to Tracie O'Keefe, 1.1.97).

WOOTTEN, J P
Statement to Martin Smith & Co, 12.9.97 (The Harper family's solicitor).

PETITION

This petition is calling for a change in the law, to prohibit the use of hypnosis for entertainment purposes. We, the undersigned, believe that this practice is dangerous and is not in the public interest.

Date	Name	Address	Signature

Please photocopy the petition, distribute it to your colleagues, friends and families. When signed, please return to: Campaign Against Stage Hypnosis (CASH), 62 Station Road, Hesketh Bank, nr Preston Lancs, PR4 6SP.

TRANS-X-U-ALL

The Naked Difference
By Tracie O'Keefe and Katrina Fox
Foreword by April Ashley

Please send me..........copies of the above book, which is a comprehensive overview of the transsexual experience. I attach payment totalling.............Cheques made payable to **EXTRAORDINARY PEOPLE PRESS**, which includes postage and packing.

NAME . . . .

Address . . . .

. . . .

Town . . . . **Zip/Post code** . . . .

Country . . . .

If you are paying by credit card please fill in the following details:

Name of card holder . . . .

Card no. . . . .

Statement address . . . .

Town . . . . **Zip/Post code** . . . .

Country . . . . **Date of card issue** . . . .

Date of expiry . . . . . **SIGNATURE** . . . .

Only VISA/DELTA/MASTERCARD CARDS ARE ACCEPTED.
Please allow 28 days for delivery. Mail to Extraordinary People Press, Suite 412 Triumph House, 185-191 Regent St, London W1R 7WB. Prices: UK £13.99/ Europe £14.99/ USA &overseas £16.99. Payment can be made by cash in £Sterling or $US and £Sterling only by UK Cheque, Eurocheque, UK Postal Order, IMO, Credit cards. This form can be faxed to 0171 439 3536 for credit card orders only.

Information at:
http://easyweb.easynet.co.uk/~katfox/

TRACIE O'KEEFE
SEMINARS AND LECTURES

Tracie is a qualified and registered clinical hypnotherapist, psychotherapist, counsellor and trainer at the London Medical Centre, Harley Street. She trained with the National School of Hypnosis and Advanced Psychotherapy in London. Her degree in Clinical Hypnotherapy was earned at the American Institute of Hypnotherapy in the USA and issued in co-ordination with the State of California. She is presently completing her doctorate with this institution. Further to this she has trained at other colleges and schools and constantly spends a lot of her time on developing her skills as a therapist. For over 20 years she has been helping people empower themselves and achieve their goals.

With a wealth of experience in the field of personal and sexual identity, she both writes and speaks on the subject. She is the internationally successful author of the book, **Trans-X-U-All: The Naked Difference**, and teaches in the field of sex, sexuality and gender in the National Health system (UK) as well as teaching communication skills to sexual health workers.

Her special project has been the development of the **Pansexual model of sex, gender and sexuality**, and her work has been reviewed in several international academic publications, including *the European Journal of Clinical Hypnosis* and *The Psychotherapist*. Far from being a stuffy lecturer she is a vibrant and engaging speaker who is fascinated and devoted to human development through therapeutic approaches combined with hypnosis.

Tracie is available for talks, seminars and workshops. For further details or enquiries, please contact her on:

Tel. 0171 439 1995 Fax. 0171 439 3536
E-mail katfox@easynet.co.uk

INVESTIGATING
Stage Hypnosis
By Tracie O'Keefe
Foreword by Margaret Harper

Please send me..........copies of the above book, which is a comprehensive overview of stage hypnosis. I attach payment totalling................Cheques made payable to **EXTRAORDINARY PEOPLE PRESS**, which includes postage and packing.

NAME . . . .

Address . . . .

. . . .

Town. . . . . **Zip/Post code** . . . .

Country. . . . .

If you are paying by credit card please fill in the following details:

Name of card holder . . . .

Card no. . . . .

Statement address . . . .

Town. . . . . **Zip/Post code** . . . .

Country. . . . . **Date of card issue** . . . .

Date of expiry. . . . . **SIGNATURE**. . . . .

Only VISA/DELTA/MASTERCARD CARDS ARE ACCEPTED.
Please allow 28 days for delivery. Mail to Extraordinary People Press, Suite 412 Triumph House, 185-191 Regent St, London W1R 7WB. Prices: UK £11.99/ Europe £12.99/ USA &overseas £14.99. Payment can be made by cash in £Sterling or $US and £Sterling only by UK Cheque, Eurocheque, UK Postal Order, IMO, Credit cards. This form can be faxed to 0171 439 3536 for credit card orders only.

Information at:
http://easyweb.easynet.co.uk/~katfox/